THE WHEELS OF CHANCE

BY THE SAME AUTHOR.

THE FOOD OF THE GODS, AND HOW IT CAME TO EARTH.
TWELVE STORIES AND A DREAM.
THE FIRST MEN IN THE MOON.
THE INVISIBLE MAN.
LOVE AND MR. LEWISHAM.
ANTICIPATIONS.
MANKIND IN THE MAKING.
A MODERN UTOPIA.
KIPPS: THE STORY OF A SIMPLE SOUL.

Frontispiece.

THE WHEELS OF CHANCE

A BICYCLING IDYLL

BY

H. G. WELLS

Author of "The Time Machine," "The Wonderful Visit," etc.

WITH ILLUSTRATIONS BY J. AYTON SYMINGTON

ISBN 978-1-4357-4986-3

To

MY DEAR MOTHER

CONTENTS

	PAGE
The Principal Character in the Story	1
The Riding Forth of Mr. Hoopdriver	17
The Shameful Episode of the Young Lady in Grey	29
On the Road to Ripley	40
How Mr. Hoopdriver was Haunted	59
The Imaginings of Mr. Hoopdriver's Heart	69
Omissions	76
The Dreams of Mr. Hoopdriver	79
How Mr. Hoopdriver went to Haslemere	84
How Mr. Hoopdriver reached Midhurst	92
An Interlude	99
Of the Artificial in Man, and of the Zeitgeist	105
The Encounter at Midhurst	109
The Pursuit	127
At Bognor	136

	PAGE
THE MOONLIGHT RIDE	157
THE SURBITON INTERLUDE	167
THE AWAKENING OF MR. HOOPDRIVER	178
THE DEPARTURE FROM CHICHESTER	185
THE UNEXPECTED ANECDOTE OF THE LION	197
THE RESCUE EXPEDITION	207
MR. HOOPDRIVER, KNIGHT ERRANT	231
THE ABASEMENT OF MR. HOOPDRIVER	256
IN THE NEW FOREST	280
AT THE RUFUS STONE	297
THE ENVOY	317

THE WHEELS OF CHANCE

THE PRINCIPAL CHARACTER IN THE STORY

I

If you (presuming you are of the sex that does such things) — if you had gone into the Drapery Emporium — which is really only magnificent for shop — of Messrs. Antrobus & Co. — a perfectly fictitious "Co.," by the bye — of Putney, on the 14th of August, 1895, had turned to the right-hand side, where the blocks of white linen and piles of blankets rise up to the rail from which the pink and blue prints depend, you might have been served by the central figure of this story that is now beginning. He would have come forward, bowing and swaying, he would have extended two hands with largish knuckles and enormous cuffs over the counter, and he would have asked you, protruding a pointed chin and without the slightest anticipation of pleasure in his manner, what he might have the pleasure of showing you. Under certain circumstances — as, for instance, hats, baby linen, gloves, silks, lace, or curtains — he would simply have bowed politely, and with a drooping expression, and making a kind of circular sweep, invited you to "step this way," and so led you beyond his ken; but under other and happier conditions, — huckaback, blankets, dimity, cretonne, linen, calico, are cases in point, — he would have requested you to take a seat, emphasising the hospitality by leaning over the counter and gripping a chair back in a spasmodic manner, and so proceeded to obtain, unfold, and exhibit his goods for your consideration. Under which happier circumstances you might — if of an observing turn of mind and not too much of a housewife to be inhuman — have given the central figure of this story less cursory attention.

Now if you had noticed anything about him, it would have been chiefly to notice how little he was noticeable. He wore the black morning coat, the black tie, and the speckled grey nether parts (descending into shadow and mystery below the counter) of his craft. He was of a pallid complexion, hair of a kind of dirty fairness, greyish eyes, and a skimpy, immature moustache under his peaked indeterminate nose. His features were all small, but none ill-shaped.

A rosette of pins decorated the lappel of his coat. His remarks, you would observe, were entirely what people used to call *cliché*, formulæ not organic to the occasion, but stereotyped ages ago and learnt years since by heart. "This, madam," he would say, "is selling very well." "We are doing a very good article at four three a yard." "We could show you something better, of course." "No trouble, madam, I assure you." Such were the simple counters of his intercourse. So, I say, he would have presented himself to your superficial observation. He would have danced about behind the counter, have neatly refolded the goods he had shown you, have put on one side those you selected, extracted a little book with a carbon leaf and a tinfoil sheet from a fixture, made you out a little bill in that weak flourishing hand peculiar to drapers, and have bawled "Sayn!" Then a puffy little shop-walker would have come into view, looked at the bill for a second, very hard (showing you a parting down the middle of his head meanwhile), have scribbled a still more flourishing J. M. all over the document, have asked you if there was nothing more, have stood by you — supposing that you were paying cash — until the central figure of this story reappeared with the change. One glance more at him, and the puffy little shop-walker would have been bowing you out, with fountains of civilities at work all about you. And so the interview would have terminated.

But real literature, as distinguished from anecdote, does not concern itself with superficial appearances alone. Literature is revelation. Modern literature is indecorous revelation. It is the duty of the earnest author to tell you what you would not have seen — even at the cost of some blushes. And the thing that you would not have seen about this young man, and the thing of the greatest moment to this story, the thing that must be told if the book is to be written, was — let us face it bravely — the Remarkable Condition of this Young Man's Legs.

Let us approach the business with dispassionate explicitness. Let us assume something of the scientific spirit, the hard, almost professorial tone of the conscientious realist. Let us treat this young man's legs as a mere diagram, and indicate the points of interest with the unemotional precision of a lecturer's pointer. And so to our revelation. On the internal aspect of the right ankle of this young man you would have observed, ladies and gentlemen, a contusion and an abrasion; on the internal aspect of the left ankle a contusion also; on its external aspect a large yellowish bruise. On his left shin there were two bruises, one a leaden yellow graduating here and there into purple, and another, obviously of more recent date, of a blotchy red—tumid and threatening. Proceeding up the left leg in a spiral manner, an unnatural hardness and redness would have been discovered on the upper aspect of the calf, and above the knee and on the inner side, an extraordinary expanse of bruised surface, a kind of closely stippled shading of contused points. The right leg would be found to be bruised in a marvellous manner all about and under the knee, and particularly on the interior aspect of the knee. So far we may proceed with our details. Fired by these discoveries, an investigator might perhaps have pursued his inquiries further—to bruises on the shoulders, elbows, and even the finger joints, of the central figure of our story. He had indeed been bumped and battered at an extraordinary number of points. But enough of realistic description is as good as a feast, and we have exhibited enough for our purpose. Even in literature one must know where to draw the line.

Now the reader may be inclined to wonder how a respectable young shopman should have got his legs, and indeed himself generally, into such a dreadful condition. One might fancy that he had been sitting with his nether extremities in some complicated machinery, a threshing-machine, say, or one of those hay-making furies. But Sherlock Holmes (now happily dead) would have fancied nothing of the kind. He would have recognised at once that the bruises on the internal aspect of the left leg, considered in the light of the distribution of the other abrasions and contusions, pointed unmistakably to the violent impact of the Mounting Beginner upon the bicycling saddle, and that the ruinous state of the right knee was equally eloquent of the concussions attendant on that person's hasty, frequently causeless, and invariably ill-conceived descents. One large bruise on the shin is even more characteristic of the 'prentice cyclist, for upon every one of them waits the jest of the unexpected treadle. You try at least to walk your machine in an easy manner, and whack!—you are rubbing your shin. So out of innocence we ripen. *Two* bruises on that place mark a certain want of aptitude in learning, such as one might expect in a person unused to muscular exercise. Blisters on the hands are eloquent of the nervous clutch of the wavering rider. And so forth, until Sherlock is presently explaining, by the help of the minor injuries, that the machine ridden is an old-fashioned affair with a fork instead of the diamond frame, a cushioned tire, well worn on the hind wheel, and a gross weight all on of perhaps three-and-forty pounds.

The revelation is made. Behind the decorous figure of the attentive shopman that I had the honour

of showing you at first, rises a vision of a nightly struggle, of two dark figures and a machine in a dark road, — the road, to be explicit, from Roehampton to Putney Hill, — and with this vision is the sound of a heel spurning the gravel, a gasping and grunting, a shouting of "Steer, man, steer!" a wavering unsteady flight, a spasmodic turning of the missile edifice of man and machine, and a collapse. Then you descry dimly through the dusk the central figure of this story sitting by the roadside and rubbing his leg at some new place, and his friend, sympathetic (but by no means depressed), repairing the displacement of the handle-bar.

Thus even in a shop assistant does the warmth of manhood assert itself, and drive him against all the conditions of his calling, against the counsels of prudence and the restrictions of his means, to seek the wholesome delights of exertion and danger and pain. And our first examination of the draper reveals beneath his draperies — the man! To which initial fact (among others) we shall come again in the end.

II

But enough of these revelations. The central figure of our story is now going along behind the counter, a draper indeed, with your purchases in his arms, to the warehouse, where the various articles you have selected will presently be packed by the senior porter and sent to you. Returning thence to his particular place, he lays hands on a folded piece of gingham, and gripping the corners of the folds in his hands, begins to straighten them punctiliously. Near him is an apprentice, apprenticed to the same high calling of draper's assistant, a ruddy, red-haired lad in a very short tailless black coat and a very high collar, who is deliberately unfolding and refolding some patterns of cretonne. By twenty-one he too may hope to be a full-blown assistant, even as Mr. Hoopdriver. Prints depend from the brass rails above them, behind are fixtures full of white packages containing, as inscriptions testify, *Lino*, *Hd Bk*, and *Mull*. You might imagine to see them that the two were both intent upon nothing but smoothness of textile and rectitude of fold. But to tell the truth, neither is thinking of the mechanical duties in hand. The assistant is dreaming of the delicious time — only four hours off now — when he will resume the tale of his bruises and abrasions. The apprentice is nearer the long long thoughts of boyhood, and his imagination rides *cap-à-pie* through the chambers of his brain, seeking some knightly quest in honour of that Fair Lady, the last but one of the girl apprentices to the dress-making upstairs. He inclines rather to street fighting against revolutionaries — because then she could see him from the window.

Jerking them back to the present comes the puffy little shop-walker, with a paper in his hand. The apprentice becomes extremely active. The shop-walker eyes the goods in hand. "Hoopdriver," he says, "how's that line of g-sez-x ginghams?"

Hoopdriver returns from an imaginary triumph over the uncertainties of dismounting. "They're going fairly well, sir. But the larger checks seem hanging."

The shop-walker brings up parallel to the counter. "Any particular time when you want your holidays?" he asks.

Hoopdriver pulls at his skimpy moustache. "No — Don't want them too late, sir, of course."

"How about this day week?"

Hoopdriver becomes rigidly meditative, gripping the corners of the gingham folds in his hands. His face is eloquent of conflicting considerations. Can he learn it in a week? That's the question. Otherwise Briggs will get next week, and he will have to wait until September — when the weather is often uncertain. He is naturally of a sanguine disposition. All drapers have to be, or else they could never have the faith they show in the beauty, washability, and unfading excellence of the goods they sell you. The decision comes at last. "That'll do me very well," said Mr. Hoopdriver, terminating the pause.

The die is cast.

The shop-walker makes a note of it and goes on to Briggs in the "dresses," the next in the strict scale of precedence of the Drapery Emporium. Mr. Hoopdriver in alternating spasms anon straightens his gingham and anon becomes meditative, with his tongue in the hollow of his decaying wisdom tooth.

III

At supper that night, holiday talk held undisputed sway. Mr. Pritchard spoke of "Scotland," Miss Isaacs clamoured of Bettws-y-Coed, Mr. Judson displayed a proprietary interest in the Norfolk Broads. "*I?*" said Hoopdriver when the question came to him. "Why, cycling, of course."

"You're never going to ride that dreadful machine of yours, day after day?" said Miss Howe of the Costume Department.

"I am," said Hoopdriver as calmly as possible, pulling at the insufficient moustache. "I'm going for a Cycling Tour. Along the South Coast."

"Well, all I hope, Mr. Hoopdriver, is that you'll get fine weather," said Miss Howe. "And not come any nasty croppers."

"And done forget some tinscher of arnica in yer bag," said the junior apprentice in the very high collar. (He had witnessed one of the lessons at the top of Putney Hill.)

"You stow it," said Mr. Hoopdriver, looking hard and threateningly at the junior apprentice, and sud-

denly adding in a tone of bitter contempt, — "Jampot."

"I'm getting fairly safe upon it now," he told Miss Howe.

At other times Hoopdriver might have further resented the satirical efforts of the apprentice, but his mind was too full of the projected Tour to admit any petty delicacies of dignity. He left the supper table early, so that he might put in a good hour at the desperate gymnastics up the Roehampton Road before it would be time to come back for locking up. When the gas was turned off for the night he was sitting on the edge of his bed, rubbing arnica into his knee — a new and very big place — and studying a Road Map of the South of England. Briggs of the "dresses," who shared the room with him, was sitting up in bed and trying to smoke in the dark. Briggs had never been on a cycle in his life, but he felt Hoopdriver's inexperience and offered such advice as occurred to him.

"Have the machine thoroughly well oiled," said Briggs, "carry one or two lemons with you, don't tear yourself to death the first day, and sit upright. Never lose control of the machine, and always sound the bell on every possible opportunity. You mind those things, and nothing very much can't happen to you, Hoopdriver — you take my word."

He would lapse into silence for a minute, save perhaps for a curse or so at his pipe, and then break out with an entirely different set of tips.

"Avoid running over dogs, Hoopdriver, whatever you do. It's one of the worst things you can do to run over a dog. Never let the machine buckle — there was a man killed only the other day through his wheel buckling — don't scorch, don't ride on the foot-path, keep your own side of the road, and if you see a tram-line, go round the corner at once, and hurry off into the next county — and always light up before dark. You mind just a few little things like that, Hoopdriver, and nothing much can't happen to you — you take my word."

"Right you are!" said Hoopdriver. "Good-night, old man."

"Good-night," said Briggs, and there was silence for a space, save for the succulent respiration of the pipe. Hoopdriver rode off into Dreamland on his machine, and was scarcely there before he was pitched back into the world of sense again. — Something — what was it?

"Never oil the steering. It's fatal," a voice that came from round a fitful glow of light, was saying. "And clean the chain daily with black-lead. You mind just a few little things like that — "

"Lord *love* us!" said Hoopdriver, and pulled the bedclothes over his ears.

THE RIDING FORTH OF MR. HOOPDRIVER

IV

ONLY those who toil six long days out of the seven, and all the year round, save for one brief glorious fortnight or ten days in the summer time, know the exquisite sensations of the First Holiday Morning. All the dreary, uninteresting routine drops from you suddenly, your chains fall about your feet. All at once you are Lord of yourself, Lord of every hour in the long, vacant day; you may go where you please, call none Sir or Madame, have a lappel free of pins, doff your black morning coat, and wear the colour of your heart, and be a Man. You grudge sleep, you grudge eating, and drinking even, their intrusion on those exquisite moments. There will be no more rising before breakfast in casual old clothing, to go dusting and getting ready in a cheerless, shutter-darkened, wrappered-up shop, no more imperious cries of, "Forward, Hoopdriver," no more hasty meals, and weary attendance on fitful old women, for ten blessed days. The first morning is by far the most glorious, for you hold your whole fortune in your hands. Thereafter, every night, comes a pang, a spectre, that will not be exorcised — the premonition of the return. The shadow of going back, of being put in the cage again for another twelve months, lies blacker and blacker across the sunlight. But on the first morning of the ten the holiday has no past, and ten days seems as good as infinity.

And it was fine, full of a promise of glorious days, a deep blue sky with dazzling piles of white cloud here and there, as though celestial haymakers had been piling the swathes of last night's clouds into cocks for a coming cartage. There were thrushes in the Richmond Road, and a lark on Putney Heath. The freshness of dew was in the air; dew or the relics of an overnight shower glittered on the leaves and grass. Hoopdriver had breakfasted early by Mrs. Gunn's complaisance. He wheeled his machine up Putney Hill, and his heart sang within him. Halfway up, a dissipated-looking black cat rushed home across the road and vanished under a gate. All the big red-brick houses behind the variegated shrubs and trees had their blinds down still, and he would not have changed places with a soul in any one of them for a hundred pounds.

He had on his new brown cycling suit — a handsome Norfolk jacket thing for 30/ — and his legs — those martyr legs — were more than consoled by thick chequered stockings, "thin in the foot, thick in the leg," for all they had endured. A neat packet of American cloth behind the saddle contained his change of raiment, and the bell and the handle-bar and the hubs and lamp, albeit a trifle freckled by wear, glittered blindingly in the rising sunlight. And at the top of the hill, after only one unsuccessful attempt, which, somehow, terminated on the green, Hoopdriver mounted, and with a stately and cautious restraint in his pace, and a dignified curvature of path, began his great Cycling Tour along the Southern Coast.

There is only one phrase to describe his course at this stage, and that is — voluptuous curves. He did not ride fast, he did not ride straight, an exacting critic might say he did not ride well — but he rode generously, opulently, using the whole road and even nibbling at the footpath. The excitement never flagged. So far he had never passed or been passed by anything, but as yet the day was young and the road was clear. He doubted his steering so much that, for the present, he had resolved to dismount at the approach of anything else upon wheels. The shadows of the trees lay very long and blue across the road, the morning sunlight was like amber fire.

At the cross-roads at the top of West Hill, where the cattle trough stands, he turned towards Kingston and set himself to scale the little bit of ascent. An early heath-keeper, in his velveteen jacket, marvelled at his efforts. And while he yet struggled, the head of a carter rose over the brow.

At the sight of him Mr. Hoopdriver, according to his previous determination, resolved to dismount. He tightened the brake, and the machine stopped dead. He was trying to think what he did with his right leg whilst getting off. He gripped the handles and released the brake, standing on the left pedal and waving his right foot in the air. Then — these things take so long in the telling — he found the machine was falling over to the right. While he was deciding upon a plan of action, gravitation appears to have been busy. He was still irresolute when he found the machine on the ground, himself kneeling upon it, and a vague feeling in his mind that again Providence had dealt harshly with his shin. This happened when he was just level with the heath-keeper. The man in the approaching cart stood up to see the ruins better.

"*That* ain't the way to get off," said the heath-keeper.

Mr. Hoopdriver picked up the machine. The handle was twisted askew again. He said something under his breath. He would have to unscrew the beastly thing.

"*That* ain't the way to get off," repeated the heath-keeper, after a silence.

"*I* know that," said Mr. Hoopdriver, testily, determined to overlook the new specimen on his shin at any cost. He unbuckled the wallet behind the saddle, to get out a screw hammer.

"If you know it ain't the way to get off — whaddyer do it for?" said the heath-keeper, in a tone of friendly controversy.

Mr. Hoopdriver got out his screw hammer and went to the handle. He was annoyed. "That's my business, I suppose," he said, fumbling with the screw. The unusual exertion had made his hands shake frightfully.

The heath-keeper became meditative, and twisted his stick in his hands behind his back. "You've broken yer 'andle, ain't yer?" he said presently. Just then the screw hammer slipped off the nut. Mr. Hoopdriver used a nasty, low word.

"They're trying things, them bicycles," said the heath-keeper, charitably. "Very trying." Mr. Hoopdriver gave the nut a vicious turn and suddenly stood up — he was holding the front wheel between his knees. "I wish," said he, with a catch in his voice, "I wish you'd leave off staring at me."

Then with the air of one who has delivered an ultimatum, he began replacing the screw hammer in the wallet.

The heath-keeper never moved. Possibly he raised his eyebrows, and certainly he stared harder than he did before. "You're pretty unsociable," he said slowly, as Mr. Hoopdriver seized the handles and stood ready to mount as soon as the cart had passed.

The indignation gathered slowly but surely. "Why don't you ride on a private road of your own if no one ain't to speak to you?" asked the heath-keeper, perceiving more and more clearly the bearing of the matter. "Can't no one make a passin' remark to you, Touchy? Ain't I good enough to speak to you? Been struck wooden all of a sudden?"

Mr. Hoopdriver stared into the Immensity of the Future. He was rigid with emotion. It was like abusing the Lions in Trafalgar Square. But the heath-keeper felt his honour was at stake.

"Don't you make no remarks to '*im*,'" said the keeper as the carter came up broadside to them. "'E's a bloomin' dook, 'e is. 'E don't converse with no one under a earl. 'E's off to Windsor, 'e is; that's why 'e's stickin' his be'ind out so haughty. Pride! Why, 'e's got so much of it, 'e has to carry some of it in that there bundle there, for fear 'e'd bust if 'e didn't ease hisself a bit—'*E*—'"

But Mr. Hoopdriver heard no more. He was hopping vigorously along the road, in a spasmodic attempt to remount. He missed the treadle once and swore viciously, to the keeper's immense delight. "Nar! Nar!" said the heath-keeper.

In another moment Mr. Hoopdriver was up, and after one terrific lurch of the machine, the heath-keeper dropped out of earshot.

Mr. Hoopdriver would have liked to look back at his enemy, but he usually twisted round and upset if he tried that. He had to imagine the indignant heath-keeper telling the carter all about it. He tried to infuse as much disdain as possible into his retreating aspect.

He drove on his sinuous way down the dip by the new mere and up the little rise to the crest of the hill that drops into Kingston Vale; and so remarkable is the psychology of cycling, that he rode all the straighter and easier because the emotions the heath-keeper had aroused relieved his mind of the constant expectation of collapse that had previously unnerved him. To ride a bicycle properly is very like a love affair; chiefly it is a matter of faith. Believe you do it, and the thing is done; doubt, and, for the life of you, you cannot.

Now you may perhaps imagine that as he rode on, his feelings towards the heath-keeper were either vindictive or remorseful,— vindictive for the aggravation or remorseful for his own injudicious display of ill temper. As a matter of fact, they were nothing of the sort. A sudden, a wonderful gratitude, possessed him. The Glory of the Holidays had resumed its sway with a sudden accession of splendour. At the crest of the hill he put his feet upon the foot-rests, and now riding moderately straight, went, with a palpitating brake, down that excellent descent. A new delight was in his eyes, quite over and above the pleasure of rushing through the keen, sweet, morning air. He reached out his thumb and twanged his bell out of sheer happiness.

"'He's a bloomin' Dook — he is!'" said Mr. Hoopdriver to himself, in a soft undertone, as he went soaring down the hill, and again, "'He's a bloomin' Dook!'" He opened his mouth in a silent laugh. It was having a decent cut did it. His social superiority had been so evident that even a man like that noticed it. No more Manchester Department for ten days! Out of Manchester, a Man. The draper Hoopdriver, the Hand, had vanished from existence. Instead was a gentleman, a man of pleasure, with a five-pound note, two sovereigns, and some silver at various convenient points of his person. At any rate as good as a Dook, if not precisely in the peerage. Involuntarily at the thought of his funds Hoopdriver's right hand left the handle and sought his breast pocket, to be immediately recalled by a violent swoop of the machine towards the cemetery. Whirroo! Just missed that half-brick! Mischievous brutes there were in the world to put such a thing in the road. Some blooming 'Arry or other! Ought to prosecute a few of these roughs, and the rest would know better. That must be the buckle of the wallet was rattling on the mud-guard. How cheerfully the wheels buzzed!

The cemetery was very silent and peaceful, but the Vale was waking, and windows rattled and squeaked up, and a white dog came out of one of the houses and yelped at him. He got off, rather breathless, at the foot of Kingston Hill, and pushed up. Halfway up, an early milk chariot rattled by him; two dirty men with bundles came hurrying down. Hoopdriver felt sure they were burglars, carrying home the swag.

It was up Kingston Hill that he first noticed a peculiar feeling, a slight tightness at his knees; but he noticed, too, at the top that he rode straighter than he did before. The pleasure of riding straight blotted out these first intimations of fatigue. A man on horseback appeared; Hoopdriver, in a tumult of soul at his own temerity, passed him. Then down the hill into Kingston, with the screw hammer, behind in the wallet, rattling against the oil can. He passed, without misadventure, a fruiterer's van and a sluggish cartload of bricks. And in Kingston Hoopdriver, with the most exquisite sensations, saw the shutters half removed from a draper's shop, and two yawning youths, in dusty old black jackets and with dirty white comforters about their necks, clearing up the planks and boxes and wrappers in the window, preparatory to dressing it out. Even so had Hoopdriver been on the previous day. But now, was he not a bloomin' Dook, palpably in the sight of common men? Then round the corner to the right — bell banged furiously — and so along the road to Surbiton.

Whoop for Freedom and Adventure! Every now and then a house with an expression of sleepy surprise would open its eye as he passed, and to the right of him for a mile or so the weltering Thames flashed and glittered. Talk of your *joie de vivre!* Albeit with a certain cramping sensation about the knees and calves slowly forcing itself upon his attention.

THE SHAMEFUL EPISODE OF THE YOUNG LADY IN GREY

V

Now you must understand that Mr. Hoopdriver was not one of your fast young men. If he had been King Lemuel, he could not have profited more by his mother's instructions. He regarded the feminine sex as something to bow to and smirk at from a safe distance. Years of the intimate remoteness of a counter leave their mark upon a man. It was an adventure for him to take one of the Young Ladies of the establishment to church on a Sunday. Few modern young men could have merited less the epithet "Dorg." But I have thought at times that his machine may have had something of the blade in its metal. Decidedly it was a machine with a past. Mr. Hoopdriver had bought it second-hand from Hare's in Putney, and Hare said it had had several owners. Second-hand was scarcely the word for it, and Hare was mildly puzzled that he should be selling such an antiquity. He said it was perfectly sound, if a little old-fashioned, but he was absolutely silent about its moral character. It may even have begun its career with a poet, say, in his glorious youth. It may have been the bicycle of a Really Bad Man. No one who has ever ridden a cycle of any kind but will witness that the things are unaccountably prone to pick up bad habits — and keep them.

It is undeniable that it became convulsed with the most violent emotions directly the Young Lady in Grey appeared. It began an absolutely unprecedented Wabble — unprecedented so far as Hoopdriver's experience went. It "showed off" — the most decadent sinuosity. It left a track like one of Beardsley's feathers. He suddenly realised, too, that his cap was loose on his head and his breath a mere remnant.

The Young Lady in Grey was also riding a bicycle. She was dressed in a beautiful bluish-grey, and the sun behind her drew her outline in gold and left the rest in shadow. Hoopdriver was dimly aware that she was young, rather slender, dark, and with a bright colour and bright eyes. Strange doubts possessed him as to the nature of her nether costume. He had heard of such things of course. French, perhaps. Her handles glittered; a jet of sunlight splashed off her bell blindingly. She was approaching the high road along an affluent from the villas of Surbiton. The roads converged slantingly. She was travelling at about the same pace as Mr. Hoopdriver. The appearances pointed to a meeting at the fork of the roads.

Hoopdriver was seized with a horrible conflict of doubts. By contrast with her he rode disgracefully. Had he not better get off at once and pretend something was wrong with his treadle? Yet even the end of getting off was an uncertainty. That last occasion on Putney Heath! On the other hand, what would happen if he kept on? To go very slow seemed the abnegation of his manhood. To crawl after a mere schoolgirl! Besides, she was not riding very fast. On the other hand, to thrust himself in front of her, consuming the road in his tendril-like advance, seemed an incivility — greed. He would leave her such a very little. His business training made him prone to bow and step aside. If only one could take one's hands off the handles, one might pass with a silent elevation of the hat, of course. But even that was a little suggestive of a funeral.

Meanwhile the roads converged. She was looking at him. She was flushed, a little thin, and had very bright eyes. Her red lips fell apart. She may have been riding hard, but it looked uncommonly like a faint smile. And the things were — yes! — *rationals!* Suddenly an impulse to bolt from the situation

became clamorous. Mr. Hoopdriver pedalled convulsively, intending to pass her. He jerked against some tin thing on the road, and it flew up between front wheel and mud-guard. He twisted round towards her. Had the machine a devil?

At that supreme moment it came across him that he would have done wiser to dismount. He gave a frantic 'whoop' and tried to get round, then, as he seemed falling over, he pulled the handles straight again and to the left by an instinctive motion, and shot behind her hind wheel, missing her by a hair's breadth. The pavement kerb awaited him. He tried to recover, and found himself jumped up on the pavement and riding squarely at a neat wooden paling. He struck this with a terrific impact and shot forward off his saddle into a clumsy entanglement. Then he began to tumble over sideways, and completed the entire figure in a sitting position on the gravel, with his feet between the fork and the stay of the machine. The concussion on the gravel shook his entire being. He remained in that position, wishing that he had broken his neck, wishing even more heartily that he had never been born. The glory of life had departed. Bloomin' Dook, indeed! These unwomanly women!

There was a soft whirr, the click of a brake, two footfalls, and the Young Lady in Grey stood holding her machine. She had turned round and come back to him. The warm sunlight now was in her face. "Are you hurt?" she said. She had a pretty, clear, girlish voice. She was really very young — quite a girl, in fact. And rode so well! It was a bitter draught.

Mr. Hoopdriver stood up at once. "Not a bit," he said, a little ruefully. He became painfully aware that large patches of gravel scarcely improve the appearance of a Norfolk suit. "I'm very sorry indeed—"

"It's my fault," she said, interrupting and so saving him on the very verge of calling her 'Miss.' (He knew 'Miss' was wrong, but it was deep-seated habit with him.) "I tried to pass you on the wrong side." Her face and eyes seemed all alive. "It's my place to be sorry."

"But it was my steering—"

"I ought to have seen you were a Novice"—with a touch of superiority. "But you rode so straight coming along there!"

She really was — dashed pretty. Mr. Hoopdriver's feelings passed the nadir. When he spoke again there was the faintest flavour of the aristocratic in his voice.

"It's my first ride, as a matter of fact. But that's no excuse for my ah! blundering—"

"Your finger's bleeding," she said, abruptly.

He saw his knuckle was barked. "I didn't feel it," he said, feeling manly.

"You don't at first. Have you any sticking-plaster? If not—" She balanced her machine against herself. She had a little side pocket, and she whipped out a small packet of sticking-plaster with a pair of scissors in a sheath at the side, and cut off a generous portion. He had a wild impulse to ask her to stick it on for him. Controlled. "Thank you," he said.

"Machine all right?" she asked, looking past him at the prostrate vehicle, her hands on her handle-bar. For the first time Hoopdriver did not feel proud of his machine.

He turned and began to pick up the fallen fabric. He looked over his shoulder, and she was gone, turned his head over the other shoulder down the road, and she was riding off. "*Orf!*" said Mr. Hoopdriver. "Well, I'm blowed!— Talk about Slap Up!" (His aristocratic refinement rarely adorned his speech in his private soliloquies.) His mind was whirling. One fact was clear. A most delightful and novel human being had flashed across his horizon and was going out of his life again. The Holiday madness was in his blood. She looked round!

At that he rushed his machine into the road, and

began a hasty ascent. Unsuccessful. Try again. Confound it, will he *never* be able to get up on the thing again? She will be round the corner in a minute. Once more. Ah! Pedal! Wabble! No! Right this time! He gripped the handles and put his head down. He would overtake her.

The situation was primordial. The Man beneath prevailed for a moment over the civilised superstructure, the Draper. He pushed at the pedals with archaic violence. So Palæolithic man may have ridden his simple bicycle of chipped flint in pursuit of his exogamous affinity. She vanished round the corner. His effort was Titanic. What should he say when he overtook her? That scarcely disturbed him at first. How fine she had looked, flushed with the exertion of riding, breathing a little fast, but elastic and active! Talk about your ladylike, homekeeping girls with complexions like cold veal! But what should he say to her? That was a bother. And he could not lift his cap without risking a repetition of his previous ignominy. She was a real Young Lady. No mistake about that! None of your blooming shop girls. (There is no greater contempt in the world than that of shop men for shop girls, unless it be that of shop girls for shop men.) Phew! This was work. A certain numbness came and went at his knees.

"May I ask to whom I am indebted?" he panted to himself, trying it over. That might do. Lucky he had a card case! A hundred a shilling — while you wait. He was getting winded. The road was certainly a bit uphill. He turned the corner and saw a long stretch of road, and a grey dress vanishing. He set his teeth. Had he gained on her at all? "Monkey on a gridiron!" yelped a small boy. Hoopdriver redoubled his efforts. His breath became audible, his steering unsteady, his pedalling positively ferocious. A drop of perspiration ran into his eye, irritant as acid. The road really was uphill beyond dispute. All his physiology began to cry out at him. A last tremendous effort brought him to the corner and showed yet another extent of shady roadway, empty save for a baker's van. His front wheel suddenly shrieked aloud. "Oh Lord!" said Hoopdriver, relaxing.

Anyhow she was not in sight. He got off unsteadily, and for a moment his legs felt like wisps of cotton. He balanced his machine against the grassy edge of the path and sat down panting. His hands were gnarled with swollen veins and shaking palpably, his breath came viscid.

"I'm hardly in training yet," he remarked. His legs had gone leaden. "I don't feel as though I'd had a mouthful of breakfast." Presently he slapped his side pocket and produced therefrom a brand-new cigarette case and a packet of Vansittart's Red Herring cigarettes. He filled the case. Then his eye fell with a sudden approval on the ornamental chequering of his new stockings. The expression in his eyes faded slowly to abstract meditation.

"She *was* a stunning girl," he said. "I wonder if I shall ever set eyes on her again. And she knew how to ride, too! Wonder what she thought of me."

The phrase 'bloomin' Dook' floated into his mind with a certain flavour of comfort.

He lit a cigarette, and sat smoking and meditating. He did not even look up when vehicles passed. It was perhaps ten minutes before he roused himself. "What rot it is! What's the good of thinking such things," he said. "I'm only a blessed draper's assistant." (To be exact, he did not say blessed. The service of a shop may polish a man's exterior ways, but the 'prentices' dormitory is an indifferent school for either manners or morals.) He stood up and began wheeling his machine towards Esher. It was going to be a beautiful day, and the hedges and trees and the open country were all glorious to his town-tired eyes. But it was a little different from the elation of his start.

"Look at the gentleman wizzer bicitle," said a nursemaid on the path to a personage in a perambulator. That healed him a little. "'Gentleman wizzer bicitle,' — 'bloomin' Dook' — I can't look so very seedy," he said to himself.

"I *wonder* — I should just like to know — "

There was something very comforting in the track of *her* pneumatic running straight and steady along the road before him. It must be hers. No other pneumatic had been along the road that morning. It was just possible, of course, that he might see her once more — coming back. Should he try and say something smart? He speculated what manner of girl she might be. Probably she was one of these here New Women. He had a persuasion the cult had been maligned. Anyhow she was a Lady. And rich people, too! Her machine couldn't have cost much under twenty pounds. His mind came round and dwelt some time on her visible self. Rational dress didn't look a bit unwomanly. However, he disdained to be one of your fortune-hunters. Then his thoughts drove off at a tangent. He would certainly have to get something to eat at the next public house.

ON THE ROAD TO RIPLEY

VI

In the fulness of time, Mr. Hoopdriver drew near the Marquis of Granby at Esher, and as he came under the railway arch and saw the inn in front of him, he mounted his machine again and rode bravely up to the doorway. Burton and biscuit and cheese he had, which, indeed, is Burton in its proper company; and as he was eating there came a middle-aged man in a drab cycling suit, very red and moist and angry in the face, and asked bitterly for a lemon squash. And he sat down upon the seat in the bar and mopped his face. But scarcely had he sat down before he got up again and stared out of the doorway.

"Damn!" said he. Then, "Damned Fool!"

"Eigh?" said Mr. Hoopdriver, looking round suddenly with a piece of cheese in his cheek.

The man in drab faced him. "I called myself a Damned Fool, sir. Have you any objections?"

"Oh!—None. None," said Mr. Hoopdriver. "I thought you spoke to me. I didn't hear what you said."

"To have a contemplative disposition and an energetic temperament, sir, is hell. Hell, I tell you. A contemplative disposition and a phlegmatic temperament, all very well. But energy and philosophy — !"

Mr. Hoopdriver looked as intelligent as he could, but said nothing.

"There's no hurry, sir, none whatever. I came out for exercise, gentle exercise, and to notice the scenery and to botanise. And no sooner do I get on the accursed machine, than off I go hammer and tongs; I never look to right or left, never notice a flower, never see a view, get hot, juicy, red, — like a grilled chop. Here I am, sir. Come from Guildford in something under the hour. *Why*, sir?"

Mr. Hoopdriver shook his head.

"Because I'm a damned fool, sir. Because I've reservoirs and reservoirs of muscular energy, and one or other of them is always leaking. It's a most interesting road, birds and trees, I've no doubt, and wayside flowers, and there's nothing I should enjoy more than watching them. But I can't. Get me on that machine, and I have to go. Get me on anything, and I have to go. And I don't want to go a bit. *Why* should a man rush about like a rocket, all pace and fizzle? Why? It makes me furious. I can assure you, sir, I go scorching along the road, and cursing aloud at myself for doing it. A quiet, dignified, philosophical man, that's what I am — at bottom; and here I am dancing with rage and swearing like a drunken tinker at a perfect stranger —

"But my day's wasted. I've lost all that country road, and now I'm on the fringe of London. And I might have loitered all the morning! Ugh! Thank Heaven, sir, you have not the irritable temperament, that you are not goaded to madness by your endogenous sneers, by the eternal wrangling of an uncomfortable soul and body. I tell you, I lead a cat and dog life — But what *is* the use of talking? — It's all of a piece!"

He tossed his head with unspeakable self-disgust, pitched the lemon squash into his mouth, paid for it, and without any further remark strode to the door. Mr. Hoopdriver was still wondering what to say when his interlocutor vanished. There was a noise of a foot spurning the gravel, and when Mr. Hoopdriver reached the doorway, the man in drab was a score of yards Londonward. He had already gathered pace. He pedalled with ill-suppressed anger, and his head was going down. In another moment he flew swiftly out of sight under the railway arch, and Mr. Hoopdriver saw him no more.

VII

AFTER this whirlwind Mr. Hoopdriver paid his reckoning and — being now a little rested about the muscles of the knees — resumed his saddle and rode on in the direction of Ripley, along an excellent but undulating road. He was pleased to find his command over his machine already sensibly increased. He set himself little exercises as he went along and performed them with variable success. There was, for instance, steering in between a couple of stones, say a foot apart, a deed of little difficulty as far as the front wheel is concerned. But the back wheel, not being under the sway of the human eye, is apt to take a vicious jump over the obstacle, which sends a violent concussion all along the spine to the skull, and will even jerk a loosely fastened hat over the eyes, and so lead to much confusion. And again, there was taking the hand or hands off the handle-bar, a thing simple in itself, but complex in its consequences. This particularly was a feat Mr. Hoopdriver desired to do, for several divergent reasons; but at present it simply led to convulsive balancings and novel and inelegant modes of dismounting.

The human nose is, at its best, a needless excrescence. There are those who consider it ornamental, and would regard a face deprived of its assistance with pity or derision; but it is doubtful whether our esteem is dictated so much by a sense of its absolute beauty as by the vitiating effect of a universally prevalent fashion. In the case of bicycle students, as in the young of both sexes, its inutility is aggravated by its persistent annoyance — it requires constant attention. Until one can ride with one hand, and search for, secure, and use a pocket handkerchief with the other, cycling is necessarily a constant series of descents. Nothing can be further from the author's ambition than a wanton realism, but Mr. Hoopdriver's nose is a plain and salient fact, and face it we must. And, in addition to this inconvenience, there are flies. Until the cyclist can steer with one hand, his face is given over to Beelzebub. Contemplative flies stroll over it, and trifle absently with its most sensitive surfaces. The only way to dislodge them is to shake the head forcibly and to writhe one's features violently. This is not only a lengthy and frequently ineffectual method, but one exceedingly terrifying to foot passengers. And again, sometimes the beginner rides for a space with one eye closed by perspiration, giving him a waggish air foreign to his mood and ill calculated to overawe the impertinent. However, you will appreciate now the motive of Mr. Hoopdriver's experiments. He presently attained sufficient dexterity to slap himself smartly and violently in the face with his right hand, without certainly overturning the machine; but his pocket handkerchief might have been in California for any good it was to him while he was in the saddle.

Yet you must not think that because Mr. Hoopdriver was a little uncomfortable, he was unhappy in the slightest degree. In the background of his consciousness was the sense that about this time Briggs would be half-way through his window dressing, and Gosling, the apprentice, busy, with a chair turned down over the counter and his ears very red, trying to roll a piece of huckaback — only those who have rolled pieces of huckaback know quite how detestable huckaback is to roll — and the shop would be dusty and, perhaps, the governor about and snappy. And here was quiet and greenery, and one mucked about as the desire took one, without a soul to see, and here was no wailing of "Sayn," no folding of remnants, no voice to shout, "Hoopdriver, forward!" And once he almost ran over something wonderful, a little, low, red beast with a yellowish tail, that went rushing across the road before him. It was the first weasel he had ever seen in his cockney life. There were miles of this, scores of miles of this before him, pinewood and oak forest, purple, heathery moorland and grassy down, lush meadows, where shining rivers wound their lazy way, villages with square-towered, flint churches, and rambling, cheap, and hearty inns, clean, white, country towns, long downhill stretches, where one might ride at one's ease (overlooking a jolt or so), and far away, at the end of it all, — the sea.

What mattered a fly or so in the dawn of these delights? Perhaps he had been dashed a minute by the shameful episode of the Young Lady in Grey, and perhaps the memory of it was making itself a little lair in a corner of his brain from which it could distress him in the retrospect by suggesting that he looked like a fool; but for the present that trouble was altogether in abeyance. The man in drab — evidently a swell — had spoken to him as his equal, and the knees of his brown suit and the chequered stockings were ever before his eyes. (Or, rather, you could see the stockings by carrying the head a little to one side.) And to feel, little by little, his mastery over this delightful, treacherous machine, growing and growing!— Every half-mile or so his knees reasserted themselves, and he dismounted and sat awhile by the roadside.

It was at a charming little place between Esher

and Cobham, where a bridge crosses a stream, that Mr. Hoopdriver came across the other cyclist in brown. It is well to notice the fact here, although the interview was of the slightest, because it happened that subsequently Hoopdriver saw a great deal more of this other man in brown. The other cyclist in brown had a machine of dazzling newness, and a punctured pneumatic lay across his knees. He was a man of thirty or more, with a whitish face, an aquiline nose, a lank, flaxen moustache, and very fair hair, and he scowled at the job before him. At the sight of him Mr. Hoopdriver pulled himself together, and rode by with the air of one born to the wheel. "A splendid morning," said Mr. Hoopdriver, "and a fine surface."

"The morning and you and the surface be everlastingly damned!" said the other man in brown as Hoopdriver receded. Hoopdriver heard the mumble and did not distinguish the words, and he felt a pleasing sense of having duly asserted the wide sympathy that binds all cyclists together, of having behaved himself as becomes one of the brotherhood of the wheel. The other man in brown watched his receding aspect. "Greasy proletarian," said the other man in brown, feeling a prophetic dislike. "Got a suit of brown, the very picture of this. One would think his sole aim in life had been to caricature me. It's Fortune's way with me. Look at his insteps on the treadles! Why does Heaven make such men?"

And having lit a cigarette, the other man in brown returned to the business in hand.

Mr. Hoopdriver worked up the hill towards Cobham to a point that he felt sure was out of sight of the other man in brown, and then he dismounted and pushed his machine; until the proximity of the village and a proper pride drove him into the saddle again.

VIII

BEYOND Cobham came a delightful incident, delightful, that is, in its beginning if a trifle indeterminate in the retrospect. It was perhaps half-way between Cobham and Ripley. Mr. Hoopdriver dropped down a little hill, where, unfenced from the road, fine mossy trees and bracken lay on either side; and looking up he saw an open country before him, covered with heather and set with pines, and a yellow road runing across it, and half a mile away perhaps, a little grey figure by the wayside waving something white. "Never!" said Mr. Hoopdriver with his hands tightening on the handles.

He resumed the treadles, staring away before him, jolted over a stone, wabbled, recovered, and began riding faster at once, with his eyes ahead. "It can't be," said Hoopdriver.

He rode his straightest, and kept his pedals spinning, albeit a limp numbness had resumed possession of his legs. "It *can't* be," he repeated, feeling every moment more assured that it *was*. "Lord! I don't know even now," said Mr. Hoopdriver (legs awhirling), and then, "Blow my legs!"

But he kept on and drew nearer and nearer, breathing hard and gathering flies like a flypaper. In the valley he was hidden. Then the road began to rise, and the resistance of the pedals grew. As he crested the hill he saw her, not a hundred yards away from him. "It's her!" he said. "It's her—right enough. It's the suit's done it,"—which was truer even than Mr. Hoopdriver thought. But now she was not waving her handkerchief, she was not even looking at him. She was wheeling her machine slowly along the road towards him, and admiring the pretty wooded hills towards Weybridge. She might have been unaware of his existence for all the recognition he got.

For a moment horrible doubts troubled Mr. Hoopdriver. Had that handkerchief been a dream? Besides which he was deliquescent and scarlet, and felt so. It must be her coquetry—the handkerchief was indisputable. Should he ride up to her and get off, or get off and ride up to her? It was as well she didn't look, because he would certainly capsize if he lifted his cap. Perhaps that was her consideration. Even as he hesitated he was upon her. She must have heard his breathing. He gripped the brake. Steady! His right leg waved in the air, and he came down heavily and staggering, but erect. She turned her eyes upon him with admirable surprise.

Mr. Hoopdriver tried to smile pleasantly, hold up his machine, raise his cap, and bow gracefully. Indeed, he felt that he did as much. He was a man singularly devoid of the minutiæ of self-consciousness, and he was quite unaware of a tail of damp hair lying across his forehead, and just clearing his eyes, and of the general disorder of his coiffure. There was an interrogative pause.

"What can I have the pleasure—" began Mr. Hoopdriver, insinuatingly. "I mean" (remembering his emancipation and abruptly assuming his most aristocratic intonation), "can I be of any assistance to you?"

The Young Lady in Grey bit her lower lip and said very prettily, "None, thank you." She glanced away from him and made as if she would proceed.

"Oh!" said Mr. Hoopdriver, taken aback and suddenly crestfallen again. It was so unexpected. He tried to grasp the situation. Was she coquetting? Or had he—?

"Excuse me, one minute," he said, as she began to wheel her machine again.

"Yes?" she said, stopping and staring a little, with the colour in her cheeks deepening.

"I should not have alighted if I had not—imagined that you—er, waved something white—" He paused.

She looked at him doubtfully. He *had* seen it! She decided that he was not an unredeemed rough taking advantage of a mistake, but an innocent soul meaning well while seeking happiness. "I *did* wave my handkerchief," she said. "I'm very sorry. I am expecting — a friend, a gentleman," — she seemed to flush pink for a minute. "He is riding a bicycle and dressed in — in brown; and at a distance, you know —"

"Oh, quite!" said Mr. Hoopdriver, bearing up in manly fashion against his bitter disappointment. "Certainly."

"I'm Awfully sorry, you know. Troubling you to dismount, and all that."

"No trouble. 'Ssure you," said Mr. Hoopdriver, mechanically and bowing over his saddle as if it was a counter. Somehow he could not find it in his heart to tell her that the man was beyond there with a punctured pneumatic. He looked back along the road and tried to think of something else to say. But the gulf in the conversation widened rapidly and hopelessly. "There's nothing further," began Mr. Hoopdriver desperately, recurring to his stock of *clichés*.

"Nothing, thank you," she said decisively. And immediately, "This *is* the Ripley road?"

"Certainly," said Mr. Hoopdriver. "Ripley is about two miles from here. According to the milestones."

"Thank you," she said warmly. "Thank you so much. I felt sure there was no mistake. And I really am Awfully sorry — "

"Don't mention it," said Mr. Hoopdriver. "Don't mention it." He hesitated and gripped his handles to mount. "It's me," he said, "ought to be sorry." Should he say it? Was it an impertinence? Anyhow! — "Not being the other gentleman, you know."

He tried a quietly insinuating smile that he knew for a grin even as he smiled it; felt she disapproved — that she despised him, was overcome with shame at her expression, turned his back upon her, and began (very clumsily) to mount. He did so with a horrible swerve, and went pedalling off, riding very badly, as he was only too painfully aware. Nevertheless, thank Heaven for the mounting! He could not see her because it was so dangerous for him to look round, but he could imagine her indignant and pitiless. He felt an unspeakable idiot. One had to be so careful what one said to Young Ladies, and he'd gone and treated her just as though she was only a Larky Girl. It was unforgivable. He always *was* a fool. You could tell from her manner she didn't think him a gentleman. One glance, and she seemed to look clear through him and all his pretence. What rot it was venturing to speak to a girl like that! With her education she was bound to see through him at once.

How nicely she spoke too! nice clear-cut words! She made him feel what slush his own accent was. And that last silly remark. What was it?—'Not being the other gentleman, you know!' No point in it. And '*gentleman!*' What *could* she be thinking of him?

But really the Young Lady in Grey had dismissed Hoopdriver from her thoughts almost before he had vanished round the corner. She had thought no ill of him. His manifest awe and admiration of her had given her not an atom of offence. But for her just now there were weightier things to think about, things that would affect all the rest of her life. She continued slowly walking her machine Londonward. Presently she stopped. "Oh! Why *doesn't* he come?" she said, and stamped her foot petulantly. Then, as if in answer, coming down the hill among the trees, appeared the other man in brown, dismounted and wheeling his machine.

HOW MR. HOOPDRIVER WAS HAUNTED

IX

As Mr. Hoopdriver rode swaggering along the Ripley road, it came to him, with an unwarrantable sense of comfort, that he had seen the last of the Young Lady in Grey. But the ill-concealed bladery of the machine, the present machinery of Fate, the *deus ex machina,* so to speak, was against him. The bicycle, torn from this attractive young woman, grew heavier and heavier, and continually more unsteady. It seemed a choice between stopping at Ripley or dying in the flower of his days. He went into the Unicorn, after propping his machine outside the door, and, as he cooled down and smoked his Red Herring cigarette while the cold meat was getting ready, he saw from the window the Young Lady in Grey and the other man in brown, entering Ripley.

They filled him with apprehension by looking at the house which sheltered him, but the sight of his bicycle, propped in a drunk and incapable attitude against the doorway, humping its rackety mud-guard and leering at them with its darkened lantern eye, drove them away — so it seemed to Mr. Hoopdriver — to the spacious swallow of the Golden Dragon. The young lady was riding very slowly, but the other man in brown had a bad puncture and was wheeling his machine. Mr. Hoopdriver noted his flaxen moustache, his aquiline nose, his rather bent shoulders, with a sudden, vivid dislike.

The maid at the Unicorn is naturally a pleasant girl, but she is jaded by the incessant incidence of cyclists, and Hoopdriver's mind, even as he conversed with her in that cultivated voice of his — of the weather, of the distance from London, and of the excellence of the Ripley road — wandered to the incomparable freshness and brilliance of the Young Lady in Grey. As he sat at meat he kept turning his head to the window to see what signs there were of that person, but the face of the Golden Dragon displayed no appreciation of the delightful morsel it had swallowed. As an incidental consequence of this distraction, Mr. Hoopdriver was for a minute greatly inconvenienced by a mouthful of mustard. After he had called for his reckoning he went, his courage being high with meat and mustard, to the door, intending to stand, with his legs wide apart and his hands deep in his pockets, and stare boldly across the road. But just then the other man in brown appeared in the gateway of the 'Golden Dragon' yard — it is one of those delightful inns that date from the coaching days — wheeling his punctured machine. He was taking it to Flambeau's, the repairer's. He looked up and saw Hoopdriver, stared for a minute, and then scowled darkly.

But Hoopdriver remained stoutly in the doorway until the other man in brown had disappeared into Flambeau's. Then he glanced momentarily at the Golden Dragon, puckered his mouth into a whistle of unconcern, and proceeded to wheel his machine into the road until a sufficient margin for mounting was secured.

Now, at that time, I say, Hoopdriver was rather desirous than not of seeing no more of the Young Lady in Grey. The other man in brown he guessed was her brother, albeit that person was of a pallid fairness, differing essentially from her rich colouring; and, besides, he felt he had made a hopeless fool of himself. But the afternoon was against him, intolerably hot, especially on the top of his head, and the virtue had gone out of his legs to digest his cold meat, and altogether his ride to Guildford was exceedingly intermittent. At times he would walk, at times lounge by the wayside, and every public house, in spite of Briggs and a sentiment of economy, meant a lemonade and a dash of bitter. (For that is

the experience of all those who go on wheels, that drinking begets thirst, even more than thirst begets drinking, until at last the man who yields becomes a hell unto himself, a hell in which the fire dieth not, and the thirst is not quenched.) Until a pennyworth of acrid green apples turned the current that threatened to carry him away. Ever and again a cycle, or a party of cyclists, would go by, with glittering wheels and softly running chains, and on each occasion, to save his self-respect, Mr. Hoopdriver descended and feigned some trouble with his saddle. Each time he descended with less trepidation.

He did not reach Guildford until nearly four o'clock, and then he was so much exhausted that he decided to put up there for the night, at the Yellow Hammer Coffee Tavern. And after he had cooled a space and refreshed himself with tea and bread and butter and jam,— the tea he drank noisily out of the saucer,— he went out to loiter away the rest of the afternoon. Guildford is an altogether charming old town, famous, so he learnt from a Guide Book, as the scene of Master Tupper's great historical novel of Stephen Langton, and it has a delightful castle, all set about with geraniums and brass plates commemorating the gentlemen who put them up, and its Guildhall is a Tudor building, very pleasant to see, and in the afternoon the shops are busy and the people

going to and fro make the pavements look bright and prosperous. It was nice to peep in the windows and see the heads of the men and girls in the drapers' shops, busy as busy, serving away. The High Street runs down at an angle of seventy degrees to the horizon (so it seemed to Mr. Hoopdriver, whose feeling for gradients was unnaturally exalted), and it brought his heart into his mouth to see a cyclist ride down it, like a fly crawling down a window pane. The man hadn't even a brake. He visited the castle early in the evening and paid his twopence to ascend the Keep.

At the top, from the cage, he looked down over the clustering red roofs of the town and the tower of the church, and then going to the southern side sat down and lit a Red Herring cigarette, and stared away south over the old bramble-bearing, fern-beset ruin, at the waves of blue upland that rose, one behind another, across the Weald, to the lazy altitudes of Hindhead and Butser. His pale grey eyes were full of complacency and pleasurable anticipation. Tomorrow he would go riding across that wide valley.

He did not notice any one else had come up the Keep after him until he heard a soft voice behind him saying: "Well, *Miss Beaumont*, here's the view." Something in the accent pointed to a jest in the name.

"It's a dear old town, brother George," answered another voice that sounded familiar enough, and turning his head, Mr. Hoopdriver saw the other man in brown and the Young Lady in Grey, with their backs towards him. She turned her smiling profile towards Hoopdriver. "Only, you know, brothers don't call their sisters — "

She glanced over her shoulder and saw Hoopdriver. "Damn!" said the other man in brown, quite audibly, starting as he followed her glance.

Mr. Hoopdriver, with a fine air of indifference, resumed the Weald. "Beautiful old town, isn't it?" said the other man in brown, after a quite perceptible pause.

"Isn't it?" said the Young Lady in Grey.

Another pause began.

"Can't get alone anywhere," said the other man in brown, looking round.

Then Mr. Hoopdriver perceived clearly that he was in the way, and decided to retreat. It was just his luck of course that he should stumble at the head of the steps and vanish with indignity. This was the third time that he'd seen *him*, and the fourth time *her*. And of course he was too big a fat-head to raise his cap to her! He thought of that at the foot of the Keep. Apparently they aimed at the South Coast just as he did. He'd get up betimes the next day and hurry off to avoid her — them, that is. It never occurred to Mr. Hoopdriver that Miss Beaumont and her brother might do exactly the same thing, and that evening, at least, the peculiarity of a brother calling his sister "Miss Beaumont" did not recur to him. He was much too preoccupied with an analysis of his own share of these encounters. He found it hard to be altogether satisfied about the figure he had cut, revise his memories as he would.

Once more quite unintentionally he stumbled upon these two people. It was about seven o'clock. He stopped outside a linen draper's and peered over the goods in the window at the assistants in torment. He could have spent a whole day happily at that. He told himself that he was trying to see how they dressed out the brass lines over their counters, in a purely professional spirit, but down at the very bottom of his heart he knew better. The customers were a secondary consideration, and it was only after the lapse of perhaps a minute that he perceived that among them was — the Young Lady in Grey! He turned away from the window at once, and saw the other man in brown standing at the edge of the pavement and regarding him with a very curious expression of face.

There came into Mr. Hoopdriver's head the curious problem whether he was to be regarded as a nuisance haunting these people, or whether they were to be regarded as a nuisance haunting him. He abandoned the solution at last in despair, quite unable to decide upon the course he should take at the next encounter, whether he should scowl savagely at the couple or assume an attitude eloquent of apology and propitiation.

THE IMAGININGS OF MR. HOOPDRIVER'S HEART

X

Mr. Hoopdriver was (in the days of this story) a poet, though he had never written a line of verse. Or perhaps romancer will describe him better. Like I know not how many of those who do the fetching and carrying of life,—a great number of them certainly, —his real life was absolutely uninteresting, and if he had faced it as realistically as such people do in Mr. Gissing's novels, he would probably have come by way of drink to suicide in the course of a year. But that was just what he had the natural wisdom not to do. On the contrary, he was always decorating his existence with imaginative tags, hopes, and poses, deliberate and yet quite effectual self-deceptions; his experiences were mere material for a romantic superstructure. If some power had given Hoopdriver the 'giftie' Burns invoked, 'to see oursels as ithers see us,' he would probably have given it away to some one else at the very earliest opportunity. His entire life,

you must understand, was not a continuous romance, but a series of short stories linked only by the general resemblance of their hero, a brown-haired young fellow commonly, with blue eyes and a fair moustache, graceful rather than strong, sharp and resolute rather than clever (cp., as the scientific books say, p. 2). Invariably this person possessed an iron will. The stories fluctuated indefinitely. The smoking of a cigarette converted Hoopdriver's hero into something entirely worldly, subtly rakish, with a humorous twinkle in the eye and some gallant sinning in the background. You should have seen Mr. Hoopdriver promenading the brilliant gardens at Earl's Court on an early-closing night. His meaning glances! (I dare not give the meaning.) Such an influence as the eloquence of a revivalist preacher would suffice to divert the story into absolutely different channels, make him a white-souled hero, a man still pure, walking untainted and brave and helpful through miry ways. The appearance of some daintily gloved frock-coated gentleman with buttonhole and eyeglass complete, gallantly attendant in the rear of customers, served again to start visions of a simplicity essentially Cromwell-like, of sturdy plainness, of a strong, silent man going righteously through the world. This day there had predominated a fine leisurely person immaculately clothed, and riding on an unexceptional machine, a mysterious person—quite unostentatious, but with accidental self-revelation of something over the common, even a "bloomin' Dook," it might be incognito, on the tour of the South Coast.

You must not think that there was any *telling* of these stories of this life-long series by Mr. Hoopdriver. He never dreamt that they were known to a soul. If it were not for the trouble, I would, I think, go back and rewrite this section from the beginning, expunging the statements that Hoopdriver was a poet and a romancer, and saying instead that he was a playwright and acted his own plays. He was not only the sole performer, but the entire audience, and the entertainment kept him almost continuously happy. Yet even that playwright comparison scarcely expresses all the facts of the case. After all, very many of his dreams never got acted at all, possibly indeed, most of them, the dreams of a solitary walk for instance, or of a tramcar ride, the dreams dreamt behind the counter while trade was slack and mechanical foldings and rollings occupied his muscles. Most of them were little dramatic situations, crucial dialogues, the return of Mr. Hoopdriver to his native village, for instance, in a well-cut holiday suit and natty gloves, the unheard asides of the rival neighbours, the delight of the old 'mater,' the intelligence —"A ten-pound rise all at once from Antrobus, mater. Whad d'yer think of that?" or again, the first whispering of love, dainty and witty and tender, to the girl he served a few days ago with sateen, or a gallant rescue of generalised beauty in distress from truculent insult or ravening dog.

So many people do this — and you never suspect it. You see a tattered lad selling matches in the street, and you think there is nothing between him and the bleakness of immensity, between him and utter abasement, but a few tattered rags and a feeble musculature. And all unseen by you a host of heaven-sent fatuities swathes him about, even, maybe, as they swathe you about. Many men have never seen their own profiles or the backs of their heads, and for the back of your own mind no mirror has been invented. They swathe him about so thickly that the pricks of fate scarce penetrate to him, or become but a pleasant titillation. And so, indeed, it is with all of us who go on living. Self-deception is the anæsthetic of life, while God is carving out our beings.

But to return from this general vivisection to Mr. Hoopdriver's imaginings. You see now how external our view has been; we have had but the slightest transitory glimpses of the drama within, of how the things looked in the magic mirror of Mr. Hoopdriver's mind. On the road to Guildford and during his encounters with his haunting fellow-cyclists the drama had presented chiefly the quiet gentleman to whom we have alluded, but at Guildford, under more varied stimuli, he burgeoned out more variously. There was the house agent's window, for instance, set him upon a charming little comedy. He would go in, make inquires about that thirty-pound house, get the key possibly and go over it — the thing would stimulate the clerk's curiosity immensely. He searched his mind for a reason for this proceeding and discovered that he was a dynamiter needing privacy. Upon that theory he procured the key, explored the house carefully, said darkly that it might suit his special needs, but that there were *others* to consult. The clerk, however, did not understand the allusion, and merely pitied him as one who had married young and paired himself to a stronger mind than his own.

This proceeding in some occult way led to the purchase of a note-book and pencil, and that started the conception of an artist taking notes. That was a little game Mr. Hoopdriver had, in congenial company, played in his still younger days — to the infinite annoyance of quite a number of respectable excursionists at Hastings. In early days Mr. Hoopdriver had been, as his mother proudly boasted, a 'bit of a drawer,' but a conscientious and normally stupid schoolmaster perceived the incipient talent and had nipped it in the bud by a series of lessons in art.

However, our principal character figured about quite happily in old corners of Guildford, and once the other man in brown, looking out of the bay window of the Earl of Kent, saw him standing in a corner by a gateway, note-book in hand, busily sketching the Earl's imposing features. At which sight the other man in brown started back from the centre of the window, so as to be hidden from him, and crouching slightly, watched him intently through the interstices of the lace curtains.

OMISSIONS

XI

Now the rest of the acts of Mr. Hoopdriver in Guildford, on the great opening day of his holidays, are not to be detailed here. How he wandered about the old town in the dusk, and up to the Hogsback to see the little lamps below and the little stars above come out one after another; how he returned through the yellow-lit streets to the Yellow Hammer Coffee Tavern and supped bravely in the commercial room — a Man among Men; how he joined in the talk about flying-machines and the possibilities of electricity, witnessing that flying-machines were "dead certain to come," and that electricity was "wonderful, wonderful"; how he went and watched the billiard playing and said, "Left 'em" several times with an oracular air; how he fell a-yawning; and how he got out his cycling map and studied it intently, — are things that find no mention here. Nor will I enlarge upon his going into the writing-room, and marking the road from London to Guildford with a fine, bright line of the reddest of red ink. In his little cyclist hand-book there is a diary, and in the diary there is an entry of these things — it is there to this day, and I cannot do better than reproduce it here to witness that this book is indeed a true one, and no lying fable written to while away an hour.

At last he fell a-yawning so much that very reluctantly indeed he set about finishing this great and splendid day. (Alas! that all days must end at last!) He got his candle in the hall from a friendly waiting-maid, and passed upward — whither a modest novelist, who writes for the family circle, dare not follow. Yet I may tell you that he knelt down at his bedside, happy and drowsy, and said, "Our Father 'chartin' heaven," even as he had learnt it by rote from his mother nearly twenty years ago. And anon when his breathing had become deep and regular, we may creep into his bedroom and catch him at his dreams. He is lying upon his left side, with his arm under the pillow. It is dark, and he is hidden; but if you could have seen his face, sleeping there in the darkness, I think you would have perceived, in spite of that treasured, thin, and straggling moustache, in spite of your memory of the coarse words he had used that day, that the man before you was, after all, only a little child asleep.

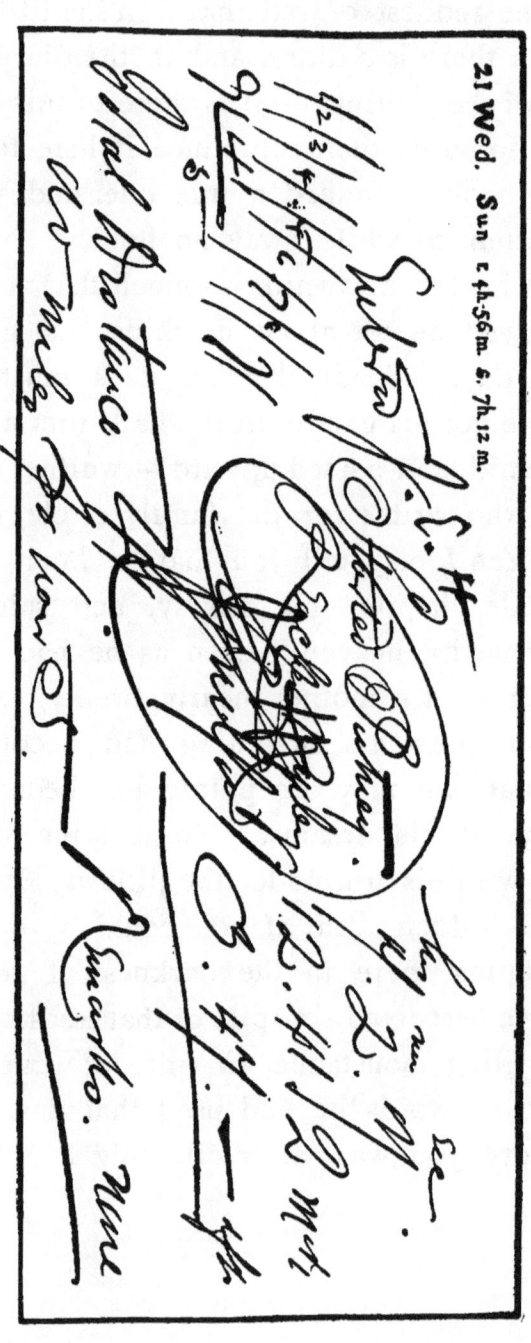

THE DREAMS OF MR. HOOPDRIVER

XII

In spite of the drawn blinds and the darkness, you have just seen Mr. Hoopdriver's face peaceful in its beauty sleep in the little, plain bedroom at the very top of the Yellow Hammer Coffee Tavern at Guildford. That was before midnight. As the night progressed he was disturbed by dreams.

After your first day of cycling one dream is inevitable. A memory of motion lingers in the muscles of your legs, and round and round they seem to go. You ride through Dreamland on wonderful dream bicycles that change and grow; you ride down steeples and staircases and over precipices; you hover in horrible suspense over inhabited towns, vainly seeking for a brake your hand cannot find, to save you from a headlong fall; you plunge into weltering rivers, and rush helplessly at monstrous obstacles. Anon Mr. Hoopdriver found himself riding out of the darkness of non-existence, pedalling Ezekiel's Wheels across the Weald of Surrey, jolting over the hills and smashing villages in his course, while the other man in brown cursed and swore at him and shouted to stop his career. There was the Putney heath-keeper, too, and the man in drab raging at him. He felt an awful fool, a — what was it? — a juggins, ah! — a Juggernaut. The villages went off one after another with a soft, squashing noise. He did not see the Young Lady in Grey, but he knew she was looking at his back. He dared not look round. Where the devil was the brake? It must have fallen off. And the bell? Right in front of him was Guildford. He tried to shout and warn the town to get out of the way, but his voice was gone as well. Nearer, nearer! it was fearful! and in another moment the houses were cracking like nuts and the blood of the inhabitants squirting this way and that. The streets were black with people running. Right under his wheels he saw the Young Lady in Grey. A feeling of horror came upon Mr. Hoopdriver; he flung himself sideways to descend, forgetting how high he was, and forthwith he began falling, falling, falling.

He woke up, turned over, saw the new moon on the window, wondered a little, and went to sleep again.

This second dream went back into the first somehow, and the other man in brown came threatening and shouting towards him. He grew uglier and uglier as he approached, and his expression was intolerably evil. He came and looked close into Mr. Hoopdriver's eyes and then receded to an incredible distance. His face seemed to be luminous. "*Miss Beaumont,*" he said, and splashed up a spray of suspicion. Some one began letting off fireworks, chiefly Catherine wheels, down the shop, though Mr. Hoopdriver knew it was against the rules. For it seemed that the place they were in was a vast shop, and then Mr. Hoopdriver perceived that the other man in brown was the shop-walker, differing from most shop-walkers in the fact that he was lit from within as a Chinese lantern might be. And the customer Mr. Hoopdriver was going to serve was the Young Lady in Grey. Curious he hadn't noticed it before. She was in grey as usual,— rationals,— and she had her bicycle leaning against the counter. She smiled quite frankly at him, just as she had done when she had apologised for stopping him. And her form, as she leant towards him, was full of a sinuous grace he had never noticed before. "What can I have the pleasure?" said Mr. Hoopdriver at once, and she said, "The Ripley road." So he got out the Ripley road and unrolled it and showed it to her, and she said that would do very nicely, and kept on looking at him and smiling, and he began measuring off eight miles by means of the yard measure on the counter, eight miles being a dress length, a rational dress length, that is; and then the other man in brown came up and wanted to interfere, and said Mr. Hoopdriver was a cad, besides measuring it off too slowly. And as Mr. Hoopdriver began to measure faster, the other man in brown said the Young Lady in Grey had been there long enough, and that he *was* her brother, or else she would not be travelling with him, and he suddenly whipped his arm about her waist and made off with her. It occurred to Mr. Hoopdriver even at the moment that this was scarcely brotherly behaviour. Of course it wasn't! The sight of the other man gripping her so familiarly enraged him frightfully; he leapt over the counter forthwith and gave chase. They ran round the shop and up an iron staircase into the Keep, and so out upon the Ripley road. For some time they kept dodging in and out of a wayside hotel with two front doors and an inn yard. The other man could not run very fast because he had hold of the Young Lady in Grey, but Mr. Hoopdriver was hampered by the absurd behaviour of his legs. They would not stretch out; they would keep going round and round as if they were on the treadles of a wheel, so that he made the smallest steps conceivable. This dream came to no crisis. The chase seemed to last an interminable time, and all kinds of people, heath-keepers, shopmen, policemen, the old man in the Keep, the angry man in drab, the barmaid at the Unicorn, men with flying-machines, people playing billiards in the doorways, silly, headless figures, stupid cocks and hens encumbered with parcels and umbrellas and waterproofs, people carrying bedroom candles, and such-like riffraff, kept getting in his way and annoying him, although he sounded his electric bell, and said, "Wonderful, wonderful!" at every corner. . . .

HOW MR. HOOPDRIVER WENT TO HASLEMERE

XIII

THERE was some little delay in getting Mr. Hoopdriver's breakfast, so that after all he was not free to start out of Guildford until just upon the stroke of nine. He wheeled his machine from the High Street in some perplexity. He did not know whether this young lady, who had seized hold of his imagination so strongly, and her unfriendly and possibly menacing brother, were ahead of him or even now breakfasting somewhere in Guildford. In the former case he might loiter as he chose; in the latter he must hurry, and possibly take refuge in branch roads.

It occurred to him as being in some obscure way strategic, that he would leave Guildford not by the obvious Portsmouth road, but by the road running through Shalford. Along this pleasant shady way he felt sufficiently secure to resume his exercises in riding with one hand off the handles, and in staring over his shoulder. He came over once or twice, but fell on his foot each time, and perceived that he was improving. Before he got to Bramley a specious byway snapped him up, ran with him for half a mile or more, and dropped him as a terrier drops a walking-stick, upon the Portsmouth again, a couple of miles from Godalming. He entered Godalming on his feet, for the road through that delightful town is beyond dispute the vilest in the world, a mere tumult of road metal, a way of peaks and precipices, and, after a successful experiment with cider at the Woolpack, he pushed on to Milford.

All this time he was acutely aware of the existence of the Young Lady in Grey and her companion in brown, as a child in the dark is of Bogies. Sometimes he could hear their pneumatics stealing upon him from behind, and looking round saw a long stretch of vacant road. Once he saw far ahead of him a glittering wheel, but it proved to be a workingman riding to destruction on a very tall ordinary. And he felt a curious, vague uneasiness about that Young Lady in Grey, for which he was altogether unable to account. Now that he was awake he had forgotten that accentuated "Miss Beaumont" that had been quite clear in his dream. But the curious dream conviction, that the girl was not really the man's sister, would not let itself be forgotten. Why, for instance, should a man want to be alone with his sister on the top of a tower?

At Milford his bicycle made, so to speak, an ass of itself. A finger-post suddenly jumped out at him, vainly indicating an abrupt turn to the right, and Mr. Hoopdriver would have slowed up and read the inscription, but no! — the bicycle would not let him. The road dropped a little into Milford, and the thing shied, put down its head and bolted, and Mr. Hoopdriver only thought of the brake when the finger-post was passed. Then to have recovered the point of intersection would have meant dismounting. For as yet there was no road wide enough for Mr. Hoopdriver to turn in. So he went on his way — or to be precise, he did exactly the opposite thing. The road to the right was the Portsmouth road, and this he was on went to Haslemere and Midhurst. By that error it came about that he once more came upon his fellow-travellers of yesterday, coming on them suddenly, without the slightest preliminary announcement and when they least expected it, under the Southwestern Railway arch. "It's horrible," said a girlish voice; "it's brutal — cowardly — " And stopped.

His expression, as he shot out from the archway at them, may have been something between a grin of recognition and a scowl of annoyance at himself for the unintentional intrusion. But disconcerted as he was, he was yet able to appreciate something of the peculiarity of their mutual attitudes. The bicycles were lying by the roadside, and the two riders stood face to face. The other man in brown's attitude, as it flashed upon Hoopdriver, was a deliberate pose; he twirled his moustache and smiled faintly, and he was conscientiously looking amused. And the girl stood rigid, her arms straight by her side, her handkerchief clenched in her hand, and her face was flushed, with the faintest touch of red upon her eyelids. She seemed to Mr. Hoopdriver's sense to be indignant. But that was the impression of a second. A mask of surprised recognition fell across this revelation of emotion as she turned her head towards him, and the pose of the other man in brown vanished too in a momentary astonishment. And then he had passed them, and was riding on towards Haslemere to make what he could of the swift picture that had photographed itself on his brain.

"Rum," said Mr. Hoopdriver. "It's *dashed* rum!"

"They were having a row."

"Smirking — " What he called the other man in brown need not trouble us.

"Annoying her!" That any human being should do that!

"*Why?*"

The impulse to interfere leapt suddenly into Mr. Hoopdriver's mind. He grasped his brake, descended, and stood looking hesitatingly back. They still stood by the railway bridge, and it seemed to Mr. Hoopdriver's fancy that she was stamping her foot. He hesitated, then turned his bicycle round, mounted, and rode back towards them, gripping his courage firmly lest it should slip away and leave him ridiculous. "I'll offer 'im a screw 'ammer," said Mr. Hoopdriver. Then, with a wave of fierce emotion, he saw that the girl was crying. In another moment they heard him and turned in surprise. Certainly she had been crying; her eyes were swimming in tears, and the other man in brown looked exceedingly disconcerted. Mr. Hoopdriver descended and stood over his machine.

"Nothing wrong, I hope?" he said, looking the other man in brown squarely in the face. "No accident?"

"Nothing," said the other man in brown shortly. "Nothing at all, thanks."

"But," said Mr. Hoopdriver, with a great effort, "the young lady is crying. I thought perhaps—"

The Young Lady in Grey started, gave Hoopdriver one swift glance, and covered one eye with her handkerchief. "It's this speck," she said. "This speck of dust in my eye."

"This lady," said the other man in brown, explaining, "has a gnat in her eye."

There was a pause. The young lady busied herself with her eye. "I believe it's out," she said. The other man in brown made movements indicating commiserating curiosity concerning the alleged fly. Mr. Hoopdriver — the word is his own — stood flabber-gastered. He had all the intuition of the simple-minded. He knew there was no fly. But the ground was suddenly cut from his feet. There is a limit to knight-errantry — dragons and false knights are all very well, but flies! Fictitious flies! Whatever the trouble was, it was evidently not his affair. He felt he had made a fool of himself again. He would have mumbled some sort of apology; but the other man in brown gave him no time, turned on him abruptly, even fiercely. "I hope," he said, "that your curiosity is satisfied?"

"Certainly," said Mr. Hoopdriver.

"Then we won't detain you."

And, ignominiously, Mr. Hoopdriver turned his machine about, struggled upon it, and resumed the road southward. And when he learnt that he was not on the Portsmouth road, it was impossible to turn and go back, for that would be to face his shame again, and so he had to ride on by Brook Street up the hill to Haslemere. And away to the right the Portsmouth road mocked at him and made off to its fastnesses amid the sunlit green and purple masses of Hindhead, where Mr. Grant Allen writes his Hill Top Novels day by day.

The sun shone, and the wide blue hill views and pleasant valleys one saw on either hand from the sand-scarred roadway, even the sides of the road itself set about with grey heather scrub and prickly masses of gorse, and pine trees with their year's growth still bright green, against the darkened needles of the previous years, were fresh and delightful to Mr. Hoopdriver's eyes. But the brightness of the day and the day-old sense of freedom fought an uphill fight against his intolerable vexation at that abominable encounter, and had still to win it when he reached Haslemere. A great brown shadow, a monstrous hatred of the other man in brown, possessed him. He had conceived the brilliant idea of abandoning Portsmouth, or at least giving up the straight way to his fellow-wayfarers, and of striking out boldly to the left, eastward. He did not dare to stop at any of the inviting public-houses in the main street of Haslemere, but turned up a side way and found a little beer-shop, the Good Hope, wherein to refresh himself. And there he ate and gossipped condescendingly with an aged labourer, assuming the while for his own private enjoyment the attributes of a Lost Heir, and afterwards mounted and rode on towards Northchapel, a place which a number of finger-posts conspired to boom, but which some insidious turning prevented him from attaining.

HOW MR. HOOPDRIVER REACHED MIDHURST

XIV

It was one of my uncle's profoundest remarks that human beings are the only unreasonable creatures. This observation was so far justified by Mr. Hoopdriver that, after spending the morning tortuously avoiding the other man in brown and the Young Lady in Grey, he spent a considerable part of the afternoon in thinking about the Young Lady in Grey, and contemplating in an optimistic spirit the possibilities of seeing her again. Memory and imagination played round her, so that his course was largely determined by the windings of the road he traversed. Of one general proposition he was absolutely convinced. "There's something Juicy wrong with 'em," said he — once even aloud. But what it was he could not imagine. He recapitulated the facts. "Miss Beaumont" — brother and sister — and the stoppage to quarrel and weep — it was perplexing material for a young man of small experience. There was no exertion he hated so much as inference, and after a time he gave up any attempt to get at the realities of the case, and let his imagination go free. Should he ever see her again? Suppose he did—with that other chap not about. The vision he found pleasantest was an encounter with her, an unexpected encounter at the annual Dancing Class 'Do' at the Putney Assembly Rooms. Somehow they would drift together, and he would dance with her again and again. It was a pleasant vision, for you must understand that Mr. Hoopdriver danced uncommonly well. Or again, in the shop, a sudden radiance in the doorway, and she is bowed towards the Manchester counter. And then to lean over that counter and murmur, seemingly *àpropos* of the goods under discussion, "I have not forgotten that morning on the Portsmouth road," and lower, "I never shall forget."

At Northchapel Mr. Hoopdriver consulted his map and took counsel and weighed his course of action. Petworth seemed a possible resting-place, or Pullborough; Midhurst seemed too near, and any place over the Downs beyond, too far, and so he meandered towards Petworth, posing himself perpetually and loitering, gathering wild flowers and wondering why they had no names—for he had never heard of any —dropping them furtively at the sight of a stranger, and generally 'mucking about.' There were purple

vetches in the hedges, meadowsweet, honeysuckle, belated brambles—but the dog-roses had already gone; there were green and red blackberries, stellarias, and dandelions, and in another place white dead nettles, traveller's-joy, clinging bedstraw, grasses flowering, white campions, and ragged robins. One cornfield was glorious with poppies, bright scarlet and purple white, and the blue corn-flowers were beginning. In the lanes the trees met overhead, and the wisps of hay still hung to the straggling hedges. In one of the main roads he steered a perilous passage through a dozen surly dun oxen. Here and there were little cottages, and picturesque beer-houses with the vivid brewers' boards of blue and scarlet, and once a broad green and a church, and an expanse of some hundred houses or so. Then he came to a pebbly rivulet that emerged between clumps of sedge loosestrife and forget-me-nots under an arch of trees, and rippled across the road, and there he dismounted, longing to take off shoes and stockings—those stylish chequered stockings were now all dimmed with dust—and paddle his lean legs in the chuckling cheerful water. But instead he sat in a manly attitude, smoking a cigarette, for fear lest the Young Lady in Grey should come glittering round the corner. For the flavour of the Young Lady in Grey was present through it all, mixing with the flowers and all the delight of it, a touch that made this second day quite different from the first, an undertone of expectation, anxiety, and something like regret that would not be ignored.

It was only late in the long evening that, quite abruptly, he began to repent, vividly and decidedly, having fled these two people. He was getting hungry, and that has a curious effect upon the emotional colouring of our minds. The man was a sinister brute, Hoopdriver saw in a flash of inspiration, and the girl — she was in some serious trouble. And he who might have helped her had taken his first impulse as decisive — and bolted. This new view of it depressed him dreadfully. What might not be happening to her now? He thought again of her tears. Surely it was merely his duty, seeing the trouble afoot, to keep his eye upon it.

He began riding fast to get quit of such self-reproaches. He found himself in a tortuous tangle of roads, and as the dusk was coming on, emerged, not at Petworth but at Easebourne, a mile from Midhurst. "I'm getting hungry," said Mr. Hoopdriver, inquiring of a gamekeeper in Easebourne village. "Midhurst a mile, and Petworth five! — Thenks, I'll take Midhurst."

He came into Midhurst by the bridge at the watermill, and up the North Street, and a little shop flourishing cheerfully, the cheerful sign of a teapot, and exhibiting a brilliant array of tobaccos, sweets, and children's toys in the window, struck his fancy. A neat, bright-eyed little old lady made him welcome, and he was presently supping sumptuously on sausages and tea, with a visitors' book full of the most humorous and flattering remarks about the little old lady, in verse and prose, propped up against his teapot as he ate. Regular good some of the jokes were, and rhymes that read well — even with your mouth full of sausage. Mr. Hoopdriver formed a vague idea of drawing "something" — for his judgment on the little old lady was already formed. He pictured the little old lady discovering it afterwards — "My gracious! One of them *Punch* men," she would say. The room had a curtained recess and a chest of drawers, for presently it was to be his bedroom, and the day part of it was decorated with framed Oddfellows' certificates and gilt-backed books and portraits, and kettle-holders, and all kinds of beautiful things made out of wool; very comfortable it was indeed. The window was lead framed and diamond paned, and through it one saw the corner of the vicarage and a pleasant hill crest, in dusky silhouette against the twilight sky. And after the sausages had ceased to be, he lit a Red Herring cigarette and went swaggering out into the twilight street. All shadowy blue between its dark brick houses, was the street, with a bright yellow window here and there and splashes of green and red where the chemist's illumination fell across the road.

AN INTERLUDE

XV

AND now let us for a space leave Mr. Hoopdriver in the dusky Midhurst North Street, and return to the two folks beside the railway bridge between Milford and Haslemere. She was a girl of eighteen, dark, fine featured, with bright eyes, and a rich, swift colour under her warm-tinted skin. Her eyes were all the brighter for the tears that swam in them. The man was thirty three or four, fair, with a longish nose overhanging his sandy flaxen moustache, pale blue eyes, and a head that struck out above and behind. He stood with his feet wide apart, his hand on his hip, in an attitude that was equally suggestive of defiance and aggression. They had watched Hoopdriver out of sight. The unexpected interruption had stopped the flood of her tears. He tugged his abundant moustache and regarded her calmly. She stood with face averted, obstinately resolved not to speak first. "Your behaviour," he said at last, "makes you conspicuous."

She turned upon him, her eyes and cheeks glowing, her hands clenched. "You unspeakable *cad*," she said, and choked, stamped her little foot, and stood panting.

"Unspeakable cad! My dear girl! Possible I *am* an unspeakable cad. Who wouldn't be — for you?"

"'Dear girl!' How *dare* you speak to me like that? *You* — "

"I would do anything — "

"*Oh!*"

There was a moment's pause. She looked squarely into his face, her eyes alight with anger and contempt, and perhaps he flushed a little. He stroked his moustache, and by an effort maintained his cynical calm. "Let us be reasonable," he said.

"Reasonable! That means all that is mean and cowardly and sensual in the world."

"You have always had it so — in your generalising way. But let us look at the facts of the case — if that pleases you better."

With an impatient gesture she motioned him to go on.

"Well," he said, — "you've eloped."

"I've left my home," she corrected, with dignity. "I left my home because it was unendurable. Because that woman — "

"Yes, yes. But the point is, you have eloped with me."

"You came with me. You pretended to be my friend. Promised to help me to earn a living by writing. It was you who said, why shouldn't a man and woman be friends? And now you dare — you dare —"

"Really, Jessie, this pose of yours, this injured innocence —"

"I will go back. I forbid you — I forbid you to stand in the way —"

"One moment. I have always thought that my little pupil was at least clear-headed. You don't know everything yet, you know. Listen to me for a moment."

"Haven't I been listening? And you have only insulted me. You who dared only to talk of friendship, who scarcely dared hint at anything beyond."

"But you took the hints, nevertheless. You knew. You *knew*. And you did not mind. *Mind!* You liked it. It was the fun of the whole thing for you. That I loved you, and could not speak to you. You played with it —"

"You have said all that before. Do you think that justifies you?"

"That isn't all. I made up my mind — Well, to make the game more even. And so I suggested to you and joined with you in this expedition of yours, invented a sister at Midhurst — I tell you, I *haven't* a sister! For one object — "

"Well?"

"To compromise you."

She started. That was a new way of putting it. For half a minute neither spoke. Then she began half defiantly: "Much I am compromised. Of course — I have made a fool of myself — "

"My dear girl, you are still on the sunny side of eighteen, and you know very little of this world. Less than you think. But you will learn. Before you write all those novels we have talked about, you will have to learn. And that's one point — " He hesitated. "You started and blushed when the man at breakfast called you Ma'am. You thought it a funny mistake, but you did not say anything because he was young and nervous — and besides, the thought of being my wife offended your modesty. You didn't care to notice it. But — you see; I gave your name as *Mrs*. Beaumont." He looked almost apologetic, in spite of his cynical pose. "*Mrs*. Beaumont," he repeated, pulling his flaxen moustache and watching the effect.

She looked into his eyes speechless. "I am learning fast," she said slowly, at last.

He thought the time had come for an emotional

attack. "Jessie," he said, with a sudden change of voice, "I know all this is mean, is villanous. But do you think that I have done all this scheming, all this subterfuge, for any other object — "

She did not seem to listen to his words. "I shall ride home," she said abruptly.

"To her?"

She winced.

"Just think," said he, "what she could say to you after this."

"Anyhow, I shall leave you now."

"Yes? And go — "

"Go somewhere to earn my living, to be a free woman, to live without conventionality — "

"My dear girl, do let us be cynical. You haven't money and you haven't credit. No one would take you in. It's one of two things: go back to your stepmother, or — trust to me."

"How *can* I?"

"Then you must go back to her." He paused momentarily, to let this consideration have its proper weight. "Jessie, I did not mean to say the things I did. Upon my honour, I lost my head when I spoke so. If you will, forgive me. I am a man. I could not help myself. Forgive me, and I promise you — "

"How can I trust you?"

"Try me. I can assure you — "

She regarded him distrustfully.

"At any rate, ride on with me now. Surely we have been in the shadow of this horrible bridge long enough."

"Oh! let me think," she said, half turning from him and pressing her hand to her brow.

"*Think!* Look here, Jessie. It is ten o'clock. Shall we call a truce until one?"

She hesitated, demanded a definition of the truce, and at last agreed.

They mounted, and rode on in silence, through the sunlight and the heather. Both were extremely uncomfortable and disappointed. She was pale, divided between fear and anger. She perceived she was in a scrape, and tried in vain to think of a way of escape. Only one tangible thing would keep in her mind, try as she would to ignore it. That was the quite irrelevant fact that his head was singularly like an albino cocoanut. He, too, felt thwarted. He felt that this romantic business of seduction was, after all, unexpectedly tame. But this was only the beginning. At any rate, every day she spent with him was a day gained. Perhaps things looked worse than they were; that was some consolation.

OF THE ARTIFICIAL IN MAN, AND OF THE ZEITGEIST

XVI

You have seen these two young people — Bechamel, by-the-bye, is the man's name, and the girl's is Jessie Milton — from the outside; you have heard them talking; they ride now side by side (but not too close together, and in an uneasy silence) towards Haslemere; and this chapter will concern itself with those curious little council chambers inside their skulls, where their motives are in session and their acts are considered and passed.

But first a word concerning wigs and false teeth. Some jester, enlarging upon the increase of bald heads and purblind people, has deduced a wonderful future for the children of men. Man, he said, was nowadays a hairless creature by forty or fifty, and for hair we gave him a wig; shrivelled, and we padded him; toothless, and lo! false teeth set in gold. Did he lose a limb, and a fine, new, artificial one was at his disposal; get indigestion, and to hand was artificial digestive fluid or bile or pancreatine, as the case might be. Complexions, too, were replaceable, spectacles superseded an inefficient eye-lens, and imperceptible false diaphragms were thrust into the failing ear. So he went over our anatomies, until, at last, he had conjured up a weird thing of shreds and patches, a simulacrum, an artificial body of a man, with but a doubtful germ of living flesh lurking somewhere in his recesses. To that, he held, we were coming.

How far such odd substitution for the body is possible need not concern us now. But the devil, speaking by the lips of Mr. Rudyard Kipling, hath it that in the case of one Tomlinson, the thing, so far as the soul is concerned, has already been accomplished. Time was when men had simple souls, desires as natural as their eyes, a little reasonable philanthropy, a little reasonable philoprogenitiveness, hunger, and a taste for good living, a decent, personal vanity, a healthy, satisfying pugnacity, and so forth. But now we are taught and disciplined for years and years, and thereafter we read and read for all the time some strenuous, nerve-destroying business permits. Pedagogic hypnotists, pulpit and platform hypnotists, book-writing hypnotists, newspaper-writing hypnotists, are at us all. This sugar you are eating, they tell us, is ink, and forthwith we reject it with infinite disgust. This black draught of unrequited toil is True Happiness, and down it goes with every symptom of pleasure. This Ibsen, they say, is dull past believing, and we yawn and stretch beyond endurance. Pardon! they interrupt, but this Ibsen is deep and delightful, and we vie with one another in an excess of entertainment. And when we open the heads of these two young people, we find, not a straightforward motive on the surface anywhere; we find, indeed, not a soul so much as an oversoul, a zeitgeist, a congestion of acquired ideas, a highway's feast of fine, confused thinking. The girl is resolute to Live Her Own Life, a phrase you may have heard before, and the man has a pretty perverted ambition to be a cynical artistic person of the very calmest description. He is hoping for the awakening of Passion in her, among other things. He knows Passion ought to awaken, from the text-books he has studied. He knows she admires his genius, but he is unaware that she does not admire his head. He is quite a distinguished art critic in London, and he met her at that celebrated lady novelist's, her stepmother, and here you have them well embarked upon the Adventure. Both are in the first stage of repentance, which consists, as you have probably found for yourself, in setting your teeth hard and saying, "I *will* go on."

Things, you see, have jarred a little, and they ride on their way together with a certain aloofness of manner that promises ill for the orthodox development of the Adventure. He perceives he was too precipitate. But he feels his honour is involved, and meditates the development of a new attack. And the girl? She is unawakened. Her motives are bookish, written by a haphazard syndicate of authors, novelists, and biographers, on her white inexperience. An artificial oversoul she is, that may presently break down and reveal a human being beneath it. She is still in that schoolgirl phase when a talkative old man is more interesting than a tongue-tied young one, and when to be an eminent mathematician, say, or to edit a daily paper, seems as fine an ambition as any girl need aspire to. Bechamel was to have helped her to attain that in the most expeditious manner, and here he is beside her, talking enigmatical phrases about passion, looking at her with the oddest expression, and once, and that was his gravest offence, offering to kiss her. At any rate he has apologised. She still scarcely realises, you see, the scrape she has got into.

THE ENCOUNTER AT MIDHURST

XVII

WE left Mr. Hoopdriver at the door of the little tea, toy, and tobacco shop. You must not think that a strain is put on coincidence when I tell you that next door to Mrs. Wardor's — that was the name of the bright-eyed, little old lady with whom Mr. Hoopdriver had stopped — is the Angel Hotel, and in the Angel Hotel, on the night that Mr. Hoopdriver reached Midhurst, were 'Mr.' and 'Miss' Beaumont, our Bechamel and Jessie Milton. Indeed, it was a highly probable thing; for if one goes through Guildford, the choice of southward roads is limited; you may go by Petersfield to Portsmouth, or by Midhurst to Chichester, in addition to which highways there is nothing for it but minor roadways to Petworth or Pulborough, and cross-cuts Brightonward. And coming to Midhurst from the north, the Angel's entrance lies yawning to engulf your highly respectable cyclists, while Mrs. Wardor's genial teapot is equally attractive to those who weigh their means in little scales. But to people unfamiliar with the Sussex roads — and such were the three persons of this story — the convergence did not appear to be so inevitable.

Bechamel, tightening his chain in the Angel yard after dinner, was the first to be aware of their reunion. He saw Hoopdriver walk slowly across the gateway, his head enhaloed in cigarette smoke, and pass out of sight up the street. Incontinently a mass of cloudy uneasiness, that had been partly dispelled during the day, reappeared and concentrated rapidly into definite suspicion. He put his screw hammer into his pocket and walked through the archway into the street, to settle the business forthwith, for he prided himself on his decision. Hoopdriver was merely promenading, and they met face to face.

At the sight of his adversary, something between disgust and laughter seized Mr. Hoopdriver and for a moment destroyed his animosity. "'Ere we are again!" he said, laughing insincerely in a sudden outbreak at the perversity of chance.

The other man in brown stopped short in Mr. Hoopdriver's way, staring. Then his face assumed an expression of dangerous civility. "Is it any information to you," he said, with immense politeness, "when I remark that you are following us?"

Mr. Hoopdriver, for some occult reason, resisted his characteristic impulse to apologise. He wanted to annoy the other man in brown, and a sentence that had come into his head in a previous rehearsal cropped up appropriately. "Since when," said Mr. Hoopdriver, catching his breath, yet bringing the question out valiantly, nevertheless, — "since when 'ave you purchased the county of Sussex?"

"May I point out," said the other man in brown, "that I object — we object not only to your proximity to us. To be frank — you appear to be following us — with an object."

"You can always," said Mr. Hoopdriver, "turn round if you don't like it, and go back the way you came."

"Oh-o!" said the other man in brown. "*That's* it! I thought as much."

"Did you?" said Mr. Hoopdriver, quite at sea, but rising pluckily to the unknown occasion. What was the man driving at?

"I see," said the other man. "I see. I half suspected — " His manner changed abruptly to a quality suspiciously friendly. "Yes — a word with you. You will, I hope, give me ten minutes."

Wonderful things were dawning on Mr. Hoopdriver. What did the other man take him for? Here at last was reality! He hesitated. Then he thought of an admirable phrase. "You 'ave some communication —"

"We'll call it a communication," said the other man.

"I can spare you the ten minutes," said Mr. Hoopdriver, with dignity.

"This way, then," said the other man in brown, and they walked slowly down the North Street towards the Grammar School. There was, perhaps, thirty seconds' silence. The other man stroked his moustache nervously. Mr. Hoopdriver's dramatic instincts were now fully awake. He did not quite understand in what *rôle* he was cast, but it was evidently something dark and mysterious. Doctor Conan Doyle, Victor Hugo, and Alexander Dumas were well within Mr. Hoopdriver's range of reading, and he had not read them for nothing.

"I will be perfectly frank with you," said the other man in brown.

"Frankness is always the best course," said Mr. Hoopdriver.

"Well, then — who the devil set you on this business?"

"Set me *on* this business?"

"Don't pretend to be stupid. Who's your employer? Who engaged you for this job?"

"Well," said Mr. Hoopdriver, confused. "No — I can't say."

"Quite sure?" The other man in brown glanced meaningly down at his hand, and Mr. Hoopdriver, following him mechanically, saw a yellow milled edge glittering in the twilight. Now your shop assistant is just above the tip-receiving class, and only just above it — so that he is acutely sensitive on the point.

Mr. Hoopdriver flushed hotly, and his eyes were angry as he met those of the other man in brown. "Stow it!" said Mr. Hoopdriver, stopping and facing the tempter.

"What!" said the other man in brown, surprised. "Eigh?" And so saying he stowed it in his breeches pocket.

"D'yer think I'm to be bribed?" said Mr. Hoopdriver, whose imagination was rapidly expanding the situation. "By Gosh! I'd follow you now — "

"My dear sir," said the other man in brown, "I beg your pardon. I misunderstood you. I really beg your pardon. Let us walk on. In your profession — "

"What have you got to say against my profession?"

"Well, really, you know. There are detectives of an inferior description — watchers. The whole class. Private Inquiry — I did not realise — I really trust you will overlook what was, after all — you must

admit — a natural indiscretion. Men of honour are not so common in the world — in any profession."

It was lucky for Mr. Hoopdriver that in Midhurst they do not light the lamps in the summer time, or the one they were passing had betrayed him. As it was, he had to snatch suddenly at his moustache and tug fiercely at it, to conceal the furious tumult of exultation, the passion of laughter, that came boiling up. Detective! Even in the shadow Bechamel saw that a laugh was stifled, but he put it down to the fact that the phrase "men of honour" amused his interlocutor. "He'll come round yet," said Bechamel to himself. "He's simply holding out for a fiver." He coughed.

"I don't see that it hurts you to tell me who your employer is."

"Don't you? I do."

"Prompt," said Bechamel, appreciatively. "Now here's the thing I want to put to you — the kernel of the whole business. You need not answer if you don't want to. There's no harm done in my telling you what I want to know. Are you employed to watch me — or Miss Milton?"

"I'm not the leaky sort," said Mr. Hoopdriver, keeping the secret he did not know with immense enjoyment. Miss Milton! That was her name. Perhaps he'd tell some more. "It's no good pumping. Is that all you're after?" said Mr. Hoopdriver.

Bechamel respected himself for his diplomatic gifts. He tried to catch a remark by throwing out a confidence. "I take it there are two people concerned in watching this affair."

"Who's the other?" said Mr. Hoopdriver, calmly, but controlling with enormous internal tension his self-appreciation. "Who's the other?" was really brilliant, he thought.

"There's my wife and *her* stepmother."

"And you want to know which it is?"

"Yes," said Bechamel.

"Well — arst 'em!" said Mr. Hoopdriver, his exultation getting the better of him, and with a pretty consciousness of repartee. "Arst 'em both."

Bechamel turned impatiently. Then he made a last effort. "I'd give a five-pound note to know just the precise state of affairs," he said.

"I told you to stow that," said Mr. Hoopdriver, in a threatening tone. And added with perfect truth and a magnificent mystery, "You don't quite understand who you're dealing with. But you will!" He spoke with such conviction that he half believed that that detective office of his in London — Baker Street, in fact — really existed.

With that the interview terminated. Bechamel

went back to the Angel, perturbed. "Hang detectives!" It wasn't the kind of thing he had anticipated at all. Hoopdriver, with round eyes and a wondering smile, walked down to where the mill waters glittered in the moonlight, and after meditating over the parapet of the bridge for a space, with occasional murmurs of, "Private Inquiry" and the like, returned, with mystery even in his paces, towards the town.

XVIII

THAT glee which finds expression in raised eyebrows and long, low whistling noises was upon Mr. Hoopdriver. For a space he forgot the tears of the Young Lady in Grey. Here was a new game!—and a real one. Mr. Hoopdriver as a Private Inquiry Agent, a Sherlock Holmes in fact, keeping these two people 'under observation.' He walked slowly back from the bridge until he was opposite the Angel, and stood for ten minutes, perhaps, contemplating that establishment and enjoying all the strange sensations of being this wonderful, this mysterious and terrible thing. Everything fell into place in his scheme. He had, of course, by a kind of instinct, assumed the disguise of a cyclist, picked up the first old crock he came across as a means of pursuit. 'No expense was to be spared.'

Then he tried to understand what it was in particular that he was observing. "My wife"—"*Her* stepmother!" Then he remembered her swimming eyes. Abruptly came a wave of anger that surprised him, washed away the detective superstructure, and left him plain Mr. Hoopdriver. This man in brown, with his confident manner, and his proffered half sovereign (damn him!) was up to no good, else why should he object to being watched? He was married! She was not his sister. He began to understand. A horrible suspicion of the state of affairs came into Mr. Hoopdriver's head. Surely it had not come to *that*. He was a detective!—he would find out. How was it to be done? He began to submit sketches on approval to himself. It required an effort before he could walk into the Angel bar. "A lemonade and bitter, please," said Mr. Hoopdriver.

He cleared his throat. "Are Mr. and Mrs. Bowlong stopping here?"

"What, a gentleman and a young lady—on bicycles?"

"Fairly young—a married couple."

"No," said the barmaid, a talkative person of ample dimensions. "There's no married couples stopping here. But there's a Mr. and Miss *Beaumont*." She spelt it for precision. "Sure you've got the name right, young man?"

"Quite," said Mr. Hoopdriver.

"Beaumont there is, but no one of the name of— What was the name you gave?"

"Bowlong," said Mr. Hoopdriver.

"No, there ain't no Bowlong," said the barmaid, taking up a glasscloth and a drying tumbler and beginning to polish the latter. "First off, I thought you might be asking for Beaumont—the names being similar. Were you expecting them on bicycles?"

"Yes—they said they *might* be in Midhurst to-night."

"P'raps they'll come presently. Beaumont's here, but no Bowlong. Sure that Beaumont ain't the name?"

"Certain," said Mr. Hoopdriver.

"It's curious the names being so alike. I thought p'raps—"

And so they conversed at some length, Mr. Hoopdriver delighted to find his horrible suspicion disposed of. The barmaid having listened awhile at the staircase volunteered some particulars of the young couple upstairs. Her modesty was much impressed by the young lady's costume, so she intimated, and Mr. Hoopdriver whispered the badinage natural to the occasion, at which she was coquettishly shocked. "There'll be no knowing which is which, in a year or two," said the barmaid. "And her manner too! She got off her machine and give it 'im to stick up against the kerb, and in she marched. 'I and my brother,' says she, 'want to stop here to-night. My brother doesn't mind what kind of room 'e 'as, but I want a room with a good view, if there's one to be got,' says she. He comes hurrying

in after and looks at her. 'I've settled the rooms,' she says, and 'e says 'damn!' just like that. I can fancy my brother letting me boss the show like that."

"I dessay you do," said Mr. Hoopdriver, "if the truth was known."

The barmaid looked down, smiled and shook her head, put down the tumbler, polished, and took up another that had been draining, and shook the drops of water into her little zinc sink.

"She'll be a nice little lot to marry," said the barmaid. "She'll be wearing the — well, b-dashes, as the sayin' is. I can't think what girls is comin' to."

This depreciation of the Young Lady in Grey was hardly to Hoopdriver's taste.

"Fashion," said he, taking up his change. "Fashion is all the go with you ladies — and always was. You'll be wearing 'em yourself before a couple of years is out."

"Nice they'd look on my figger," said the barmaid, with a titter. "No — I ain't one of your fashionable sort. Gracious no! I shouldn't feel as if I'd anything on me, not more than if I'd forgot — Well, there! I'm talking." She put down the glass abruptly. "I dessay I'm old fashioned," she said, and walked humming down the bar.

"Not you," said Mr. Hoopdriver. He waited until he caught her eye, then with his native courtesy smiled, raised his cap, and wished her good evening.

XIX

THEN Mr. Hoopdriver returned to the little room with the lead-framed windows where he had dined, and where the bed was now comfortably made, sat down on the box under the window, stared at the moon rising on the shining vicarage roof, and tried to collect his thoughts. How they whirled at first! It was past ten, and most of Midhurst was tucked away in bed, some one up the street was learning the violin, at rare intervals a belated inhabitant hurried home and woke the echoes, and a corncrake kept up a busy churning in the vicarage garden. The sky was deep blue, with a still luminous afterglow along the black edge of the hill, and the white moon overhead, save for a couple of yellow stars, had the sky to herself.

At first his thoughts were kinetic, of deeds and not relationships. There was this malefactor, and his victim, and it had fallen on Mr. Hoopdriver to take a hand in the game. *He* was married. Did she know he was married? Never for a moment did a thought of evil concerning her cross Hoopdriver's mind. Simple-minded people see questions of morals so much better than superior persons — who have read and thought themselves complex to impotence. He had heard her voice, seen the frank light in her eyes, and she had been weeping — that sufficed. The rights of the case he hadn't properly grasped. But he would. And that smirking — well, swine was the mildest for him. He recalled the exceedingly unpleasant incident of the railway bridge. "Thin we won't detain yer, thenks," said Mr. Hoopdriver, aloud, in a strange, unnatural, contemptible voice, supposed to represent that of Bechamel. "Oh, the *beggar!* I'll be level with him yet. He's afraid of us detectives — that I'll *swear.*" (If Mrs. Wardor should chance to be on the other side of the door within earshot, well and good.)

For a space he meditated chastisements and revenges, physical impossibilities for the most part, — Bechamel staggering headlong from the impact of Mr. Hoopdriver's large, but, to tell the truth, ill supported fist, Bechamel's five feet nine of height lifted from the ground and quivering under a vigorously applied horsewhip. So pleasant was such dreaming, that Mr. Hoopdriver's peaked face under the moonlight was transfigured. One might have paired him with that well-known and universally admired triumph, 'The Soul's Awakening,' so sweet was his ecstasy. And presently with his thirst for revenge glutted by six or seven violent assaults, a duel and two vigorous murders, his mind came round to the Young Lady in Grey again.

She was a plucky one too. He went over the incident the barmaid at the Angel had described to him. His thoughts ceased to be a torrent, smoothed down to a mirror in which she was reflected with infinite clearness and detail. He'd never met anything like her before. Fancy that bolster of a barmaid being dressed in that way! He whuffed a contemptuous laugh. He compared her colour, her vigour, her voice, with the Young Ladies in Business with whom his lot had been cast. Even in tears she was beautiful, more beautiful indeed to him, for it made her seem softer and weaker, more accessible. And such weeping as he had seen before had been so much a matter of damp white faces, red noses, and hair coming out of curl. Your draper's assistant becomes something of a judge of weeping, because weeping is the custom of all Young Ladies in Business, when for any reason their services are dispensed with. She could weep — and (by Gosh!) she could smile. *He* knew that, and reverting to acting abruptly, he smiled confidentially at the puckered pallor of the moon.

It is difficult to say how long Mr. Hoopdriver's pensiveness lasted. It seemed a long time before his thoughts of action returned. Then he remembered he was a 'watcher'; that to-morrow he must be busy. It would be in character to make notes, and he pulled out his little note-book. With that in hand he fell a-thinking again. Would that chap tell her the 'tecks were after them? If so, would she be as anxious to get away as *he* was? He must be on the alert. If possible he must speak to her. Just a significant word, "Your friend — trust me!" — It occurred to him that to-morrow these fugitives might rise early to escape. At that he thought of the time and found it was half-past eleven. "Lord!" said he, "I must see that I wake." He yawned and rose. The blind was up, and he pulled back the little chintz curtains to let the sunlight strike across to the bed, hung his watch within good view of his pillow, on a nail that supported a kettle-holder, and sat down on his bed to undress. He lay awake for a little while thinking of the wonderful possibilities of the morrow, and thence he passed gloriously into the wonderland of dreams.

THE PURSUIT

XX

AND now to tell of Mr. Hoopdriver, rising with the sun, vigilant, active, wonderful, the practicable half of the lead-framed window stuck open, ears alert, an eye flickering incessantly in the corner panes, in oblique glances at the Angel front. Mrs. Wardor wanted him to have his breakfast downstairs in her kitchen, but that would have meant abandoning the watch, and he held out strongly. The bicycle, *cap-à-pie*, occupied, under protest, a strategic position in the shop. He was expectant by six in the morning. By nine horrible fears oppressed him that his quest had escaped him, and he had to reconnoitre the Angel yard in order to satisfy himself. There he found the ostler (How are the mighty fallen in these decadent days!) brushing down the bicycles of the chase, and he returned relieved to Mrs. Wardor's premises. And about ten they emerged, and rode quietly up the North Street. He watched them until they turned the corner of the post office, and then out into the

road and up after them in fine style! They went by the engine-house where the old stocks and the whipping posts are, and on to the Chichester road, and he followed gallantly. So this great chase began.

They did not look round, and he kept them just within sight, getting down if he chanced to draw closely upon them round a corner. By riding vigorously he kept quite conveniently near them, for they made but little hurry. He grew hot indeed, and his knees were a little stiff to begin with, but that was all. There was little danger of losing them, for a thin chalky dust lay upon the road, and the track of her tire was milled like a shilling, and his was a chequered ribbon along the way. So they rode by Cobden's monument and through the prettiest of villages, until at last the downs rose steeply ahead. There they stopped awhile at the only inn in the place, and Mr. Hoopdriver took up a position which commanded the inn door, and mopped his face and thirsted and smoked a Red Herring cigarette. They remained in the inn for some time. A number of chubby innocents returning home from school, stopped and formed a line in front of him, and watched him quietly but firmly for the space of ten minutes or so. "Go away," said he, and they only seemed quietly interested. He asked them all their names then, and they answered indistinct murmurs. He gave it up at last and became passive on his gate, and so at length they tired of him.

The couple under observation occupied the inn so long that Mr. Hoopdriver at the thought of their possible employment hungered as well as thirsted. Clearly, they were lunching. It was a cloudless day, and the sun at the meridian beat down upon the top of Mr. Hoopdriver's head, a shower bath of sunshine, a huge jet of hot light. It made his head swim. At last they emerged, and the other man in brown looked back and saw him. They rode on to the foot of the down, and dismounting began to push tediously up that long nearly vertical ascent of blinding white road, Mr. Hoopdriver hesitated. It might take them twenty minutes to mount that. Beyond was empty downland perhaps for miles. He decided to return to the inn and snatch a hasty meal.

At the inn they gave him biscuits and cheese and a misleading pewter measure of sturdy ale, pleasant under the palate, cool in the throat, but leaden in the legs, of a hot afternoon. He felt a man of substance as he emerged in the blinding sunshine, but even by the foot of the down the sun was insisting again that his skull was too small for his brains. The hill had gone steeper, the chalky road blazed like a magnesium light, and his front wheel began an apparently incurable squeaking. He felt as a man from Mars would feel if he were suddenly transferred to this planet, about three times as heavy as he was wont to feel. The two little black figures had vanished over the forehead of the hill. "The tracks'll be all right," said Mr. Hoopdriver.

That was a comforting reflection. It not only justified a slow progress up the hill, but at the crest a sprawl on the turf beside the road, to contemplate the Weald from the south. In a matter of two days he had crossed that spacious valley, with its frozen surge of green hills, its little villages and townships here and there, its copses and cornfields, its ponds and streams like jewelery of diamonds and silver glittering in the sun. The North Downs were hidden, far away beyond the Wealden Heights. Down below was the little village of Cocking, and half-way up the hill, a mile perhaps to the right, hung a flock of sheep grazing together. Overhead an anxious peewit circled against the blue, and every now and then emitted its feeble cry. Up here the heat was tempered by a pleasant breeze. Mr. Hoopdriver was possessed by unreasonable contentment; he lit himself a cigarette and lounged more comfortably. Surely the Sussex ale is made of the waters of Lethe, of poppies and pleasant dreams. Drowsiness coiled insidiously about him.

He awoke with a guilty start, to find himself sprawling prone on the turf with his cap over one eye. He

sat up, rubbed his eyes, and realised that he had slept. His head was still a trifle heavy. And the chase? He jumped to his feet and stooped to pick up his overturned machine. He whipped out his watch and saw that it was past two o'clock. "Lord love us, fancy that!—But the tracks'll be all right," said Mr. Hoopdriver, wheeling his machine back to the chalky road. "I must scorch till I overtake them."

He mounted and rode as rapidly as the heat and a lingering lassitude permitted. Now and then he had to dismount to examine the surface where the road forked. He enjoyed that rather. "Trackin'," he said aloud, and decided in the privacy of his own mind that he had a wonderful instinct for 'spoor.' So he came past Goodwood station and Lavant, and approached Chichester towards four o'clock. And then came a terrible thing. In places the road became hard, in places were the crowded indentations of a recent flock of sheep, and at last in the throat of the town cobbles and the stony streets branching east, west, north, and south, at a stone cross under the shadow of the cathedral the tracks vanished. "O Cricky!" said Mr. Hoopdriver, dismounting in dismay and standing agape. "Dropped anything?" said an inhabitant at the kerb. "Yes," said Mr. Hoopdriver, "I've lost the spoor," and walked upon his way, leaving the inhabitant marvelling what part of a bicycle a spoor might be. Mr. Hoopdriver, abandoning tracking, began asking people if they had seen a Young Lady in Grey on a bicycle. Six casual people hadn't, and he began to feel the inquiry was conspicuous, and desisted. But what was to be done?

Hoopdriver was hot, tired, and hungry, and full of the first gnawings of a monstrous remorse. He decided to get himself some tea and meat, and in the Royal George he meditated over the business in a melancholy frame enough. They had passed out of his world—vanished, and all his wonderful dreams of some vague, crucial interference collapsed like a castle of cards. What a fool he had been not to stick to them like a leech! He might have thought! But there!—what *was* the good of that sort of thing now? He thought of her tears, of her helplessness, of the bearing of the other man in brown, and his wrath and disappointment surged higher. "What *can* I do?" said Mr. Hoopdriver aloud, bringing his fist down beside the teapot.

What would Sherlock Holmes have done? Perhaps, after all, there might be such things as clues in the world, albeit the age of miracles was past. But to look for a clue in this intricate network of cobbled streets, to examine every muddy interstice! There was a chance by looking about and inquiry at the various inns. Upon that he began. But of course they might have ridden straight through and scarcely a soul have marked them. And then came a positively brilliant idea. " 'Ow many ways are there out of Chichester?" said Mr. Hoopdriver. It was really equal to Sherlock Holmes — that. " If they've made tracks, I shall find those tracks. If not — they're in the town." He was then in East Street, and he started at once to make the circuit of the place, discovering incidentally that Chichester is a walled city. In passing, he made inquiries at the Black Swan, the Crown, and the Red Lion Hotel. At six o'clock in the evening, he was walking downcast, intent, as one who had dropped money, along the road towards Bognor, kicking up the dust with his shoes and fretting with disappointed pugnacity. A thwarted, crestfallen Hoopdriver it was, as you may well imagine. And then suddenly there jumped upon his attention — a broad line ribbed like a shilling, and close beside it one chequered, that ever and again split into two. " Found!" said Mr. Hoopdriver and swung round on his heel at once, and back to the Royal George, helter skelter, for the bicycle they were minding for him. The ostler thought he was confoundedly imperious, considering his machine.

AT BOGNOR

XXI

THAT seductive gentleman, Bechamel, had been working up to a crisis. He had started upon this elopement in a vein of fine romance, immensely proud of his wickedness, and really as much in love as an artificial oversoul can be, with Jessie. But either she was the profoundest of coquettes or she had not the slightest element of Passion (with a large P) in her composition. It warred with all his ideas of himself and the feminine mind to think that under their flattering circumstances she really could be so vitally deficient. He found her persistent coolness, her more or less evident contempt for himself, exasperating in the highest degree. He put it to himself that she was enough to provoke a saint, and tried to think that was piquant and enjoyable, but the blisters on his vanity asserted themselves. The fact is, he was, under this standing irritation, getting down to the natural man in himself for once, and the natural man in himself, in spite of Oxford and the

Junior Reviewers' Club, was a Palæolithic creature of simple tastes and violent methods. "I'll be level with you yet," ran like a plough through the soil of his thoughts.

Then there was this infernal detective. Bechamel had told his wife he was going to Davos to see Carter. To that he had fancied she was reconciled, but how she would take this exploit was entirely problematical. She was a woman of peculiar moral views, and she measured marital infidelity largely by its proximity to herself. Out of her sight, and more particularly out of the sight of the other women of her set, vice of the recognised description was, perhaps, permissible to those contemptible weaklings, men, but this was Evil on the High Roads. She was bound to make a fuss, and these fusses invariably took the final form of a tightness of money for Bechamel. Albeit, and he felt it was heroic of him to resolve so, it was worth doing if it was to be done. His imagination worked on a kind of matronly Valkyrie, and the noise of pursuit and vengeance was in the air. The idyll still had the front of the stage. That accursed detective, it seemed, had been thrown off the scent, and that, at any rate, gave a night's respite. But things must be brought to an issue forthwith.

By eight o'clock in the evening, in a little dining-room in the Vicuna Hotel, Bognor, the crisis had come, and Jessie, flushed and angry in the face and with her heart sinking, faced him again for her last struggle with him. He had tricked her this time, effectually, and luck had been on his side. She was booked as Mrs. Beaumont. Save for her refusal to enter their room, and her eccentricity of eating with unwashed hands, she had so far kept up the appearances of things before the waiter. But the dinner was grim enough. Now in turn she appealed to his better nature and made extravagant statements of her plans to fool him.

He was white and vicious by this time, and his anger quivered through his pose of brilliant wickedness.

"I will go to the station," she said. "I will go back —"

"The last train for anywhere leaves at 7.42."

"I will appeal to the police —"

"You don't know them."

"I will tell these hotel people."

"They will turn you out of doors. You're in such a thoroughly false position now. They don't understand — unconventionality, down here."

She stamped her foot. "If I wander about the streets all night —" she said.

"You who have never been out alone after dusk?

Do you know what the streets of a charming little holiday resort are like —"

"I don't care," she said. "I can go to the clergyman here."

"He's a charming man. Unmarried. And men are really more alike than you think. And anyhow —"

"Well?"

"How *can* you explain the last two nights to anyone now? The mischief is done, Jessie."

"You *cur*," she said, and suddenly put her hand to her breast. He thought she meant to faint, but she stood, with the colour gone from her face.

"No," he said. "I love you."

"Love!" said she.

"Yes — love."

"There are ways yet," she said, after a pause.

"Not for you. You are too full of life and hope yet for, what is it? — not the dark arch nor the black flowing river. Don't you think of it. You'll only shirk it when the moment comes, and turn it all into comedy."

She turned round abruptly from him and stood looking out across the parade at the shining sea over which the afterglow of day fled before the rising moon. He maintained his attitude. The blinds were still up, for she had told the waiter not to draw them. There was silence for some moments.

At last he spoke in as persuasive a voice as he could summon. "Take it sensibly, Jessie. Why should we, who have so much in common, quarrel into melodrama? I swear I love you. You are all that is bright and desirable to me. I am stronger than you, older; man to your woman. To find *you* too — conventional!"

She looked at him over her shoulder, and he noticed with a twinge of delight how her little chin came out beneath the curve of her cheek.

"*Man!*" she said. "Man to *my* woman! Do *men* lie? Would a *man* use his five and thirty years' experience to outwit a girl of seventeen? Man to my woman indeed! That surely is the last insult!"

"Your repartee is admirable, Jessie. I should say they do, though — all that and more also when their hearts were set on such a girl as yourself. For God's sake drop this shrewishness! Why should you be so — difficult to me? Here am I with *my* reputation, *my* career, at your feet. Look here, Jessie — on my honour, I will marry you — "

"God forbid," she said, so promptly that she never learnt he had a wife, even then. It occurred to him then for the first time, in the flash of her retort, that she did not know he was married.

"'Tis only a pre-nuptial settlement," he said, following that hint.

He paused.

"You must be sensible. The thing's your own doing. Come out on the beach now — the beach here is splendid, and the moon will soon be high."

"*I won't*," she said, stamping her foot.

"Well, well —"

"Oh! leave me alone. Let me think —"

"Think," he said, "if you want to. It's your cry always. But you can't save yourself by thinking, my dear girl. You can't save yourself in any way now. If saving it is — this parsimony —"

"Oh, go — go."

"Very well. I will go. I will go and smoke a cigar. And think of you, dear. . . . But do you think I should do all this if I did not care?"

"Go," she whispered, without glancing round. She continued to stare out of the window. He stood looking at her for a moment, with a strange light in his eyes. He made a step towards her. "I *have* you," he said. "You are mine. Netted — caught. But mine." He would have gone up to her and laid his hand upon her, but he did not dare to do that yet. "I have you in my hand," he said, "in my power. Do you hear — *Power!*"

She remained impassive. He stared at her for half a minute, and then, with a superb gesture that was lost upon her, went to the door. Surely the instinctive abasement of her sex before Strength was upon his side. He told himself that his battle was won. She heard the handle move and the catch click as the door closed behind him.

XXII

AND now without in the twilight behold Mr. Hoopdriver, his cheeks hot, his eye bright! His brain is in a tumult. The nervous, obsequious Hoopdriver, to whom I introduced you some days since, has undergone a wonderful change. Ever since he lost that 'spoor' in Chichester, he has been tormented by the most horrible visions of the shameful insults that may be happening. The strangeness of new surroundings has been working to strip off the habitual servile from him. Here was moonlight rising over the memory of a red sunset, dark shadows and glowing orange lamps, beauty somewhere mysteriously rapt away from him, tangible wrong in a brown suit and an unpleasant face, flouting him. Mr. Hoopdriver for the time was in the world of Romance and Knight-errantry, divinely forgetful of his social position or hers; forgetting, too, for the time any of the wretched timidities that had tied him long since behind the counter in his proper place. He was angry and adventurous. It was all about him, this vivid drama he had fallen into, and it was eluding him. He was far too grimly in earnest to pick up that lost thread and make a play of it now. The man was living. He did not pose when he alighted at the coffee tavern even, nor when he made his hasty meal.

As Bechamel crossed from the Vicuna towards the esplanade, Hoopdriver, disappointed and exasperated, came hurrying round the corner from the Temperance Hotel. At the sight of Bechamel, his heart jumped, and the tension of his angry suspense exploded into, rather than gave place to, an excited activity of mind. They were at the Vicuna, and she was there now alone. It was the occasion he sought. But he would give Chance no chance against him. He went back round the corner, sat down on the seat, and watched Bechamel recede into the dimness up the esplanade, before he got up and walked into the hotel entrance. "A lady cyclist in grey," he asked for, and followed boldly on the waiter's heels. The door of the dining-room was opening before he felt a qualm. And then suddenly he was nearly minded to turn and run for it, and his features seemed to him to be convulsed.

She turned with a start, and looked at him with something between terror and hope in her eyes.

"Can I — have a few words — with you, alone?" said Mr. Hoopdriver, controlling his breath with difficulty. She hesitated, and then motioned the waiter to withdraw.

Mr. Hoopdriver watched the door shut. He had intended to step out into the middle of the room, fold his arms and say, "You are in trouble. I am a Friend. Trust me." Instead of which he stood panting and then spoke with sudden familiarity, hastily, guiltily: "Look here. I don't know what the Juice is up, but I think there's something wrong. Excuse my intruding — if it isn't so. I'll do anything you like to help you out of the scrape — if you're in one. That's my meaning, I believe. What can I do? I would do anything to help you."

Her brow puckered, as she watched him make, with infinite emotion, this remarkable speech. "*You!*" she said. She was tumultuously weighing possibilities in her mind, and he had scarcely ceased when she had made her resolve.

She stepped a pace forward. "You are a gentleman," she said.

"Yes," said Mr. Hoopdriver.

"Can I trust you?"

She did not wait for his assurance. "I must leave this hotel at once. Come here."

She took his arm and led him to the window. "You can just see the gate. It is still open.

Through that are our bicycles. Go down, get them out, and I will come down to you. Dare you?"

"Get your bicycle out in the road?"

"Both. Mine alone is no good. At once. Dare you?"

"Which way?"

"Go out by the front door and round. I will follow in one minute."

"Right!" said Mr. Hoopdriver, and went.

He had to get those bicycles. Had he been told to go out and kill Bechamel he would have done it. His head was a Maëlstrom now. He walked out of the hotel, along the front, and into the big, black-shadowed coach yard. He looked round. There were no bicycles visible. Then a man emerged from the dark, a short man in a short, black, shiny jacket. Hoopdriver was caught. He made no attempt to turn and run for it. "I've been giving your machines a wipe over, sir," said the man, recognising the suit, and touching his cap. Hoopdriver's intelligence now was a soaring eagle; he swooped on the situation at once. "That's right," he said, and added, before the pause became marked, "Where is mine? I want to look at the chain."

The man led him into an open shed, and went fumbling for a lantern. Hoopdriver moved the lady's machine out of his way to the door, and then laid hands on the man's machine and wheeled it out of the shed into the yard. The gate stood open and beyond was the pale road and a clump of trees black in the twilight. He stooped and examined the chain with trembling fingers. How was it to be done? Something behind the gate seemed to flutter. The man must be got rid of anyhow.

"I say," said Hoopdriver, with an inspiration, "can you get me a screwdriver?"

The man simply walked across the shed, opened and shut a box, and came up to the kneeling Hoopdriver with a screwdriver in his hand. Hoopdriver felt himself a lost man. He took the screwdriver with a tepid "Thanks," and incontinently had another inspiration.

"I say," he said again.

"Well?"

"This is Miles too big."

The man lit the lantern, brought it up to Hoopdriver and put it down on the ground. "Want a smaller screwdriver?" he said.

Hoopdriver had his handkerchief out and sneezed a prompt *atichew*. It is the orthodox thing when you wish to avoid recognition. "As small as you have," he said, out of his pocket handkerchief.

"I ain't got none smaller than that," said the ostler.

"Won't do, really," said Hoopdriver, still wallowing in his handkerchief.

"I'll see wot they got in the 'ouse, if you like, sir," said the man. "If you would," said Hoopdriver. And as the man's heavily nailed boots went clattering down the yard, Hoopdriver stood up, took a noiseless step to the lady's machine, laid trembling hands on its handle and saddle, and prepared for a rush.

The scullery door opened momentarily and sent a beam of warm, yellow light up the road, shut again behind the man, and forthwith Hoopdriver rushed the machines towards the gate. A dark grey form came fluttering to meet him. "Give me this," she said, "and bring yours."

He passed the thing to her, touched her hand in the darkness, ran back, seized Bechamel's machine, and followed.

The yellow light of the scullery door suddenly flashed upon the cobbles again. It was too late now to do anything but escape. He heard the ostler shout behind him, and came into the road. She was up and dim already. He got into the saddle without a blunder. In a moment the ostler was in the gateway with a full-throated "*Hi!* sir! That ain't allowed;" and Hoopdriver was overtaking the Young Lady in Grey. For some moments the earth seemed alive with shouts of, "Stop 'em!" and the shadows with ambuscades of police. The road swept round, and they were riding out of sight of the hotel, and behind dark hedges, side by side.

She was weeping with excitement as he overtook her. "Brave," she said, "brave!" and he ceased to feel like a hunted thief. He looked over his shoulder and about him, and saw that they were already out of Bognor — for the Vicuna stands at the very westernmost extremity of the sea front — and riding on a fair wide road.

XXIII

THE ostler (being a fool) rushed violently down the road vociferating after them. Then he returned panting to the Vicuna Hotel, and finding a group of men outside the entrance, who wanted to know what was *up*, stopped to give them the cream of the adventure. That gave the fugitives five minutes. Then pushing breathlessly into the bar, he had to make it clear to the barmaid what the matter was, and the 'gov'nor' being out, they spent some more precious time wondering 'what — *ever*' was to be done! in which the two customers returning from outside joined with animation. There were also moral remarks and other irrelevant contributions. There were conflicting ideas of telling the police and pursuing the flying couple on a horse. That made ten minutes. Then Stephen, the waiter, who had shown Hoopdriver up, came down and lit wonderful lights and started quite a fresh discussion by the simple question "*Which?*" That turned ten minutes into a quarter of an hour. And in the midst of this discussion, making a sudden and awe-stricken silence,

appeared Bechamel in the hall beyond the bar, walked with a resolute air to the foot of the staircase, and passed out of sight. You conceive the backward pitch of that exceptionally shaped cranium? Incredulous eyes stared into one another's in the bar, as his paces, muffled by the stair carpet, went up to the landing, turned, reached the passage and walked into the dining-room overhead.

"It wasn't that one at all, miss," said the ostler, "I'd *swear.*"

"Well, that's Mr. Beaumont," said the barmaid, "— anyhow."

Their conversation hung comatose in the air, switched up by Bechamel. They listened together. His feet stopped. Turned. Went out of the dining-room. Down the passage to the bedroom. Stopped again.

"Poor chap!" said the barmaid. "She's a wicked woman!"

"Sssh!" said Stephen.

After a pause Bechamel went back to the dining-room. They heard a chair creak under him. Interlude of conversational eyebrows.

"I'm going up," said Stephen, "to break the melancholy news to him."

Bechamel looked up from a week-old newspaper as, without knocking, Stephen entered. Bechamel's face suggested a different expectation. "Beg pardon, sir," said Stephen, with a diplomatic cough.

"Well?" said Bechamel, wondering suddenly if Jessie had kept some of her threats. If so, he was in for an explanation. But he had it ready. She was a monomaniac. "Leave me alone with her," he would say; "I know how to calm her."

"Mrs. Beaumont," said Stephen.

"*Well?*"

"Has gone."

He rose with a fine surprise. "Gone!" he said with a half laugh.

"Gone, sir. On her bicycle."

"On her bicycle! Why?"

"She went, sir, with Another Gentleman."

This time Bechamel was really startled. "An — other Gentlemen! *Who?*"

"Another gentleman in brown, sir. Went into the yard, sir, got out the two bicycles, sir, and went off, sir — about twenty minutes ago."

Bechamel stood with his eyes round and his knuckle on his hips. Stephen, watching him with immense enjoyment, speculated whether this abandoned husband would weep or curse, or rush off at once in furious pursuit. But as yet he seemed merely stunned.

"Brown clothes?" he said. "And fairish?"

"A little like yourself, sir, — in the dark. The ostler, sir, Jim Duke —"

Bechamel laughed awry. Then, with infinite fervour, he said — But let us put in blank cartridge — he said, " —— —— !"

"I might have thought!"

He flung himself into the armchair.

"Damn her," said Bechamel, for all the world like a common man. "I'll chuck this infernal business! They've gone, eigh?"

"Yessir."

"Well, let 'em GO," said Bechamel, making a memorable saying. "Let 'em GO. Who cares? And I wish him luck. And bring me some Bourbon as fast as you can, there's a good chap. I'll take that, and then I'll have another look round Bognor before I turn in."

Stephen was too surprised to say anything but "Bourbon, sir?"

"Go on," said Bechamel. "Damn you!"

Stephen's sympathies changed at once. "Yessir," he murmured, fumbling for the door handle, and left the room, marvelling. Bechamel, having in this way satisfied his sense of appearances, and comported himself as a Pagan should, so soon as the waiter's footsteps had passed, vented the cream of his feelings in a stream of blasphemous indecency. Whether his wife or *her* stepmother had sent the detective, *she* had evidently gone off with him, and that little business was over. And he was here, stranded and sold, an ass, and as it were, the son of many generations of asses. And his only ray of hope was that it seemed more probable, after all, that the girl had escaped through her stepmother. In which case the business might be hushed up yet, and the evil hour of explanation with his wife indefinitely postponed. Then abruptly the image of that lithe figure in grey knickerbockers went frisking across his mind again, and he reverted to his blasphemies. He started up in a gusty frenzy with a vague idea of pursuit, and incontinently sat down again with a concussion that stirred the bar below to its depths. He banged the arms of the chair with his fist, and swore again. "Of all the accursed fools that were ever spawned," he was chanting, "I, Bechamel — " when with an abrupt tap and prompt opening of the door, Stephen entered with the Bourbon.

THE MOONLIGHT RIDE

XXIV

AND so the twenty minutes' law passed into infinity. We leave the wicked Bechamel clothing himself with cursing as with a garment, — the wretched creature has already sufficiently sullied our modest but truthful pages, — we leave the eager little group in the bar of the Vicuna Hotel, we leave all Bognor as we have left all Chichester and Midhurst and Haslemere and Guildford and Ripley and Putney, and follow this dear fool of a Hoopdriver of ours and his Young Lady in Grey out upon the moonlight road. How they rode! How their hearts beat together and their breath came fast, and how every shadow was anticipation and every noise pursuit! For all that flight Mr. Hoopdriver was in the world of Romance. Had a policeman intervened because their lamps were not lit, Hoopdriver had cut him down and ridden on, after the fashion of a hero born. Had Bechamel arisen in the way with rapiers for a duel, Hoopdriver had fought as one to whom Agincourt was a reality and drapery a dream. It was Rescue, Elopement, Glory! And she by the side of him! He had seen her face in shadow, with the morning sunlight tangled in her hair, he had seen her sympathetic with that warm light in her face, he had seen her troubled and her eyes bright with tears. But what light is there lighting a face like hers, to compare with the soft glamour of the midsummer moon?

The road turned northward, going round through the outskirts of Bognor, in one place dark and heavy under a thick growth of trees, then amidst villas again, some warm and lamplit, some white and sleeping in the moonlight; then between hedges, over which they saw broad wan meadows shrouded in a low-lying mist. They scarcely heeded whither they rode at first, being only anxious to get away, turning once westward when the spire of Chichester cathedral rose suddenly near them out of the dewy night, pale and intricate and high. They rode, speaking little, just a rare word now and then, at a turning, at a footfall, at a roughness in the road.

She seemed to be too intent upon escape to give much thought to him, but after the first tumult of the adventure, as flight passed into mere steady riding, his mind became an enormous appreciation of the position. The night was a warm white silence save for the subtile running of their chains. He looked sideways at her as she sat beside him with her ankles gracefully ruling the treadles. Now the road turned westward, and she was a dark grey outline against the shimmer of the moon; and now they faced northwards, and the soft cold light passed caressingly over her hair and touched her brow and cheek.

There is a magic quality in moonshine; it touches all that is sweet and beautiful, and the rest of the night is hidden. It has created the fairies, whom the sunlight kills, and fairyland rises again in our hearts at the sight of it, the voices of the filmy route, and their faint, soul-piercing melodies. By the moonlight every man, dull clod though he be by day, tastes something of Endymion, takes something of the youth and strength of Endymion, and sees the dear white goddess shining at him from his Lady's eyes. The firm substantial daylight things become ghostly and elusive, the hills beyond are a sea of unsubstantial texture, the world a visible spirit, the spiritual within us rises out of its darkness, loses something of its weight and body, and swims up towards heaven. This road that was a mere rutted white dust, hot underfoot, blinding to the eye, is now a soft grey silence, with the glitter of a crystal grain set starlike in its silver here and there. Overhead, riding serenely through the spacious blue, is the mother of the silence, she who has spiritualised the world, alone save for two attendant steady shining stars. And in silence under her benign influence, under the benediction of her light, rode our two wanderers side by side through the transfigured and transfiguring night.

Nowhere was the moon shining quite so brightly as in Mr. Hoopdriver's skull. At the turnings of the road he made his decisions with an air of profound promptitude (and quite haphazard). "The Right," he would say. Or again "The Left," as one who knew. So it was that in the space of an hour they came abruptly down a little lane, full tilt upon the sea. Grey beach to the right of them and to the left, and a little white cottage fast asleep inland of a sleeping fishing-boat. "'Ullo!" said Mr. Hoopdriver, *sotto voce*. They dismounted abruptly. Stunted oaks and thorns rose out of the haze of moonlight that was tangled in the hedge on either side.

"You are safe," said Mr. Hoopdriver, sweeping off his cap with an air and bowing courtly.

"Where are we?"

"*Safe.*"

"But *where?*"

"Chichester Harbour." He waved his arm seaward as though it was a goal.

"Do you think they will follow us?"

"We have turned and turned again."

It seemed to Hoopdriver that he heard her sob. She stood dimly there, holding her machine, and he, holding his, could go no nearer to her to see if she sobbed for weeping or for want of breath. "What are we to do now?" her voice asked.

"Are you tired?" he asked.

"I will do what has to be done."

The two black figures in the broken light were silent for a space. "Do you know," she said, "I am not afraid of you. I am sure you are honest to me. And I do not even know your name!"

He was taken with a sudden shame of his homely patronymic. "It's an ugly name," he said. "But you are right in trusting me. I would — I would do anything for you. . . . This is nothing."

She caught at her breath. She did not care to ask why. But compared with Bechamel! — "We take each other on trust," she said. "Do you want to know — how things are with me?

"That man," she went on, after the assent of his listening silence, "promised to help and protect me. I was unhappy at home — never mind why. A stepmother — Idle, unoccupied, hindered, cramped, that is enough, perhaps. Then he came into my life, and talked to me of art and literature, and set my brain on fire. I wanted to come out into the world, to be a human being — not a thing in a hutch. And he — "

"I know," said Hoopdriver.

"And now, here I am—"

"I will do anything," said Hoopdriver.

She thought. "You cannot imagine my stepmother. No! I could not describe her—"

"I am entirely at your service. I will help you with all my power."

"I have lost an Illusion and found a Knight-errant." She spoke of Bechamel as the Illusion.

Mr. Hoopdriver felt flattered. But he had no adequate answer.

"I'm thinking," he said, full of a rapture of protective responsibility, "what we had best be doing. You are tired, you know. And we can't wander all night — after the day we've had."

"That was Chichester we were near?" she asked.

"If," he meditated, with a tremble in his voice, "you would make *me* your brother, *Miss Beaumont.*"

"Yes?"

"We could stop there together—"

She took a minute to answer. "I am going to light these lamps," said Hoopdriver. He bent down to his own, and struck a match on his shoe. She looked at his face in its light, grave and intent. How could she ever have thought him common or absurd?

"But you must tell me your name—brother," she said.

"Er — Carrington," said Mr. Hoopdriver, after a momentary pause. Who would be Hoopdriver on a night like this?

"But the Christian name?"

"Christian name? *My* Christian name. Well — Chris." He snapped his lamp and stood up. "If you will hold my machine, I will light yours," he said.

She came round obediently and took his machine, and for a moment they stood face to face. "My name, brother Chris," she said, "is Jessie."

He looked into her eyes, and his excitement seemed arrested. "*Jessie,*" he repeated slowly. The mute emotion of his face affected her strangely. She had to speak. "It's not such a very wonderful name, is it?" she said, with a laugh to break the intensity.

He opened his mouth and shut it again, and, with a sudden wincing of his features, abruptly turned and bent down to open the lantern in front of her machine. She looked down at him, almost kneeling in front of her, with an unreasonable approbation in her eyes. It was, as I have indicated, the hour and season of the full moon.

XXV

Mr. Hoopdriver conducted the rest of that night's journey with the same confident dignity as before, and it was chiefly by good luck and the fact that most roads about a town converge thereupon, that Chichester was at last attained. It seemed at first as though everyone had gone to bed, but the Red Hotel still glowed yellow and warm. It was the first time Hoopdriver had dared the mysteries of a 'first-class' hotel. But that night he was in the mood to dare anything.

"So you found your Young Lady at last," said the ostler of the Red Hotel; for it chanced he was one of those of whom Hoopdriver had made inquiries in the afternoon.

"Quite a misunderstanding," said Hoopdriver, with splendid readiness. "My sister had gone to Bognor But I brought her back here. I've took a fancy to this place. And the moonlight's simply dee-vine."

"We've had supper, thenks, and we're tired," said Mr. Hoopdriver. "I suppose you won't take anything,—Jessie?"

The glory of having her, even as a sister! and to call her Jessie like that! But he carried it off splendidly, as he felt himself bound to admit. "Good-night, Sis," he said, "and pleasant dreams. I'll just 'ave a look at this paper before I turn in." But this was living indeed! he told himself.

So gallantly did Mr. Hoopdriver comport himself up to the very edge of the Most Wonderful Day of all. It had begun early, you will remember, with a vigil in a little sweetstuff shop next door to the Angel at Midhurst. But to think of all the things that had happened since then! He caught himself in the middle of a yawn, pulled out his watch, saw the time was half-past eleven, and marched off, with a fine sense of heroism, bedward.

THE SURBITON INTERLUDE

XXVI

AND here, thanks to the glorious institution of sleep, comes a break in the narrative again. These absurd young people are safely tucked away now, their heads full of glowing nonsense, indeed, but the course of events at any rate is safe from any fresh developments through their activities for the next eight hours or more. They are both sleeping healthily you will perhaps be astonished to hear. Here is the girl — what girls are coming to nowadays only Mrs. Lynn Linton can tell! — in company with an absolute stranger, of low extraction and uncertain accent, unchaperoned and unabashed; indeed, now she fancies she is safe, she is, if anything, a little proud of her own share in these transactions. Then this Mr. Hoopdriver of yours, roseate idiot that he is! is in illegal possession of a stolen bicycle, a stolen young lady, and two stolen names, established with them in an hotel that is quite beyond his means, and immensely proud of himself in a somnolent way for these incomparable follies. There are occasions when a moralising novelist can merely wring his hands and leave matters to take their course. For all Hoopdriver knows or cares he may be locked up the very first thing to-morrow morning for the rape of the cycle. Then in Bognor, let alone that melancholy vestige, Bechamel (with whom our dealings are, thank Goodness! over), there is a Coffee Tavern with a steak Mr. Hoopdriver ordered, done to a cinder long ago, his American-cloth parcel in a bedroom, and his own proper bicycle, by way of guarantee, carefully locked up in the hayloft. To-morrow he will be a Mystery, and they will be looking for his body along the sea front. And so far we have never given a glance at the desolate home in Surbiton, familiar to you no doubt through the medium of illustrated interviews, where the unhappy stepmother —

That stepmother, it must be explained, is quite well known to you. That is a little surprise I have prepared for you. She is 'Thomas Plantagenet,' the gifted authoress of that witty and daring book, "A Soul Untrammelled," and quite an excellent woman in her way, — only it is such a crooked way. Her real name is Milton. She is a widow and a charming one, only ten years older than Jessie, and she is always careful to dedicate her more daring works to the 'sacred memory of my husband' to show that there's nothing personal, you know, in the matter. Considering her literary reputation (she was always speaking of herself as one 'martyred for truth,' because the critics advertised her written indecorums in column long 'slates'), — considering her literary reputation, I say, she was one of the most respectable women it is possible to imagine. She furnished correctly, dressed correctly, had severe notions of whom she might meet, went to church, and even at times took the sacrament in some esoteric spirit. And Jessie she brought up so carefully that she never even let her read "A Soul Untrammelled." Which, therefore, naturally enough, Jessie did, and went on from that to a feast of advanced literature. Mrs. Milton not only brought up Jessie carefully, but very slowly, so that at seventeen she was still a clever schoolgirl (as you have seen her) and quite in the background of the little literary circle of unimportant celebrities which 'Thomas Plantagenet' adorned. Mrs. Milton knew Bechamel's reputation of being a dangerous man; but then bad men are not bad women, and she let him come to her house to show she was not afraid — she took no account of Jessie. When the elopement came, therefore, it was a double disappointment to her, for she perceived his hand by a kind of instinct.

She did the correct thing. The correct thing, as you know, is to take hansom cabs, regardless of expense, and weep and say you do not know *what* to do, round the circle of your confidential friends. She could not have ridden nor wept more had Jessie been her own daughter — she showed the properest spirit. And she not only showed it, but felt it.

Mrs. Milton, as a successful little authoress and still more successful widow of thirty-two, — "Thomas Plantagenet is a charming woman," her reviewers used to write invariably, even if they spoke ill of her, — found the steady growth of Jessie into womanhood an unmitigated nuisance and had been willing enough to keep her in the background. And Jessie — who had started this intercourse at fourteen with abstract objections to stepmothers — had been active enough in resenting this. Increasing rivalry and antagonism had sprung up between them, until they could engender quite a vivid hatred from a dropped hairpin or the cutting of a book with a sharpened knife. There is very little deliberate wickedness in the world. The stupidity of our selfishness gives much the same results indeed, but in the ethical laboratory it shows a different nature. And when the disaster came, Mrs. Milton's remorse for their gradual loss of sympathy and her share in the losing of it, was genuine enough.

You may imagine the comfort she got from her friends, and how West Kensington and Notting Hill and Hampstead, the literary suburbs, those decent penitentiaries of a once Bohemian calling, hummed with the business. Her 'Men'—as a charming literary lady she had, of course, an organised corps —were immensely excited, and were sympathetic; helpfully energetic, suggestive, alert, as their ideals of their various dispositions required them to be. "Any news of Jessie?" was the pathetic opening of a dozen melancholy but interesting conversations. To her Men she was not perhaps so damp as she was to her women friends, but in a quiet way she was even more touching. For three days, Wednesday that is, Thursday, and Friday, nothing was heard of the fugitives. It was known that Jessie, wearing a patent costume with button-up skirts, and mounted on a diamond frame safety with Dunlops, and a loofah covered saddle, had ridden forth early in the morning, taking with her about two pounds seven shillings in money, and a grey touring case packed, and there, save for a brief note to her stepmother, —a declaration of independence, it was said, an assertion of her Ego containing extensive and very annoying quotations from "A Soul Untrammelled," and giving no definite intimation of her plans—knowledge ceased. That note was shown to few, and then only in the strictest confidence.

But on Friday evening late came a breathless Man Friend, Widgery, a correspondent of hers, who had heard of her trouble among the first. He had been touring in Sussex, — his knapsack was still on his back, — and he testified hurriedly that at a place called Midhurst, in the bar of an hotel called the Angel, he had heard from a barmaid a vivid account of a Young Lady in Grey. Descriptions tallied. But who was the man in brown? "The poor, misguided girl! I must go to her at once," she said, choking, and rising with her hand to her heart.

"It's impossible to-night. There are no more trains. I looked on my way."

"A mother's love," she said. "I bear her *that*."

"I know you do." He spoke with feeling, for no one admired his photographs of scenery more than Mrs. Milton. "It's more than she deserves."

"Oh, don't speak unkindly of her! She has been misled."

It was really very friendly of him. He declared he was only sorry his news ended there. Should he follow them, and bring her back? He had come to her because he knew of her anxiety. "It is *good* of you," she said, and quite instinctively took and pressed his hand. "And to think of that poor girl

— to-night! It's dreadful." She looked into the fire that she had lit when he came in, the warm light fell upon her dark purple dress, and left her features in a warm shadow. She looked such a slight, frail thing to be troubled so. "We must follow her." Her resolution seemed magnificent. "I have no one to go with me."

"He must marry her," said the man.

"She has no friends. We have no one. After all — Two women. So helpless."

And this fair-haired little figure was the woman that people who knew her only from her books, called bold, prurient even! Simply because she was great-hearted — intellectual. He was overcome by the unspeakable pathos of her position.

"Mrs. Milton," he said. "Hetty!"

She glanced at him. The overflow was imminent. "Not now," she said, "not now. I must find her first."

"Yes," he said with intense emotion. (He was one of those big, fat men who feel deeply.) "But let me help you. At least let me help you."

"But can you spare time?" she said. "For *me*."

"For you —"

"But what can I do? what can *we* do?"

"Go to Midhurst. Follow her on. Trace her. She was there on Thursday night, last night. She

cycled out of the town. Courage!" he said. "We will save her yet!"

She put out her hand and pressed his again.

"Courage!" he repeated, finding it so well received.

There were alarms and excursions without. She turned her back to the fire, and he sat down suddenly in the big armchair, which suited his dimensions admirably. Then the door opened, and the girl showed in Dangle, who looked curiously from one to the other. There was emotion here, he had heard the armchair creaking, and Mrs. Milton, whose face was flushed, displayed a suspicious alacrity to explain. "You, too," she said, "are one of my good friends. And we have news of her at last."

It was decidedly an advantage to Widgery, but Dangle determined to show himself a man of resource. In the end he, too, was accepted for the Midhurst Expedition, to the intense disgust of Widgery; and young Phipps, a callow youth of few words, faultless collars, and fervent devotion, was also enrolled before the evening was out. They would scour the country, all three of them. She appeared to brighten up a little, but it was evident she was profoundly touched. She did not know what she had done to merit such friends. Her voice broke a little, she moved towards the door, and young Phipps, who was a youth of action rather than of words, sprang and opened it — proud to be first.

"She is sorely troubled," said Dangle to Widgery.

"We must do what we can for her."

"She is a wonderful woman," said Dangle. "So subtle, so intricate, so many faceted. She feels this deeply."

Young Phipps said nothing, but he felt the more.

And yet they say the age of chivalry is dead!

But this is only an Interlude, introduced to give our wanderers time to refresh themselves by good, honest sleeping. For the present, therefore, we will not concern ourselves with the starting of the Rescue Party, nor with Mrs. Milton's simple but becoming grey dress, with the healthy Widgery's Norfolk jacket and thick boots, with the slender Dangle's energetic bearing, nor with the wonderful chequerings that set off the legs of the golf-suited Phipps. They are after us. In a little while they will be upon us. You must imagine as you best can the competitive raidings at Midhurst of Widgery, Dangle, and Phipps. How Widgery was great at questions, and Dangle good at inference, and Phipps so conspicuously inferior in everything that he felt it, and sulked with Mrs. Milton most of the day, after the manner of your callow youth the whole world over. Mrs. Milton stopped at the Angel and was very sad and charming and intelligent, and Widgery paid the bill. In the afternoon of Saturday, Chichester was attained. But by that time our fugitives — As you shall immediately hear.

THE AWAKENING OF MR. HOOPDRIVER

XXVII

MR. HOOPDRIVER stirred on his pillow, opened his eyes, and, staring unmeaningly, yawned. The bedclothes were soft and pleasant. He turned the peaked nose that overrides the insufficient moustache, up to the ceiling, a pinkish projection over the billow of white. You might see it wrinkle as he yawned again, and then become quiet. So matters remained for a space. Very slowly recollection returned to him. Then a shock of indeterminate brown hair appeared, and first one watery grey eye a-wondering, and then two; the bed upheaved, and you had him, his thin neck projecting abruptly from the clothes he held about him, his face staring about the room. He held the clothes about him, I hope I may explain, because his night-shirt was at Bognor in an American-cloth packet, derelict. He yawned a third time, rubbed his eyes, smacked his lips. He was recalling almost everything now. The pursuit, the hotel, the tremulous daring of his entry, the swift adventure of the inn yard, the moonlight — Abruptly he threw the clothes back and rose into a sitting position on the edge of the bed. Without was the noise of shutters being unfastened and doors unlocked, and the passing of hoofs and wheels in the street. He looked at his watch. Half-past six. He surveyed the sumptuous room again.

"Lord!" said Mr. Hoopdriver. "It wasn't a dream, after all."

"I wonder what they charge for these Juicèd rooms!" said Mr. Hoopdriver, nursing one rosy foot.

He became meditative, tugging at his insufficient moustache. Suddenly he gave vent to a noiseless laugh. "What a rush it was! Rushed in and off with his girl right under his nose. Planned it well too. Talk of highway robbery! Talk of brigands! Up and off! How juicèd *sold* he must be feeling! It was a shave too — in the coach yard!"

Suddenly he became silent. Abruptly his eyebrows rose and his jaw fell. "I sa—a—ay!" said Mr. Hoopdriver.

He had never thought of it before. Perhaps you will understand the whirl he had been in overnight. But one sees things clearer in the daylight. "I'm hanged if I haven't been and stolen a blessed bicycle."

"Who cares?" said Mr. Hoopdriver, presently, and his face supplied the answer.

Then he thought of the Young Lady in Grey again, and tried to put a more heroic complexion on the business. But of an early morning, on an empty stomach (as with characteristic coarseness, medical men put it) heroics are of a more difficult growth than by moonlight. Everything had seemed exceptionally fine and brilliant, but quite natural, the evening before.

Mr. Hoopdriver reached out his hand, took his Norfolk jacket, laid it over his knees, and took out the money from the little ticket pocket. "Fourteen and six-half," he said, holding the coins in his left hand and stroking his chin with his right. He verified, by patting, the presence of a pocketbook in the breast pocket. "Five, fourteen, six-half," said Mr. Hoopdriver. "Left."

With the Norfolk jacket still on his knees, he plunged into another silent meditation. "That wouldn't matter," he said. "It's the bike's the bother.

"No good going back to Bognor.

"Might send it back by carrier, of course. Thanking him for the loan. Having no further use — " Mr. Hoopdriver chuckled and lapsed into the silent concoction of a delightfully impudent letter. "Mr.

J. Hoopdriver presents his compliments." But the grave note reasserted itself.

"Might trundle back there in an hour, of course, and exchange them. *My* old crock's so blessed shabby. He's sure to be spiteful too. Have me run in, perhaps. Then she'd be in just the same old fix, only worse. You see, I'm her Knight-errant. It complicates things so."

His eye, wandering loosely, rested on the sponge bath. "What the juice do they want with cream pans in a bedroom?" said Mr. Hoopdriver, *en passant.*

"Best thing we can do is to set out of here as soon as possible, anyhow. I suppose she'll go home to her friends. That bicycle is a juicy nuisance, anyhow. Juicy nuisance!"

He jumped to his feet with a sudden awakening of energy, to proceed with his toilet. Then with a certain horror he remembered that the simple necessaries of that process were at Bognor! "Lord!" he remarked, and whistled silently for a space. "Rummy go! profit and loss; profit, one sister with bicycle complete, wot offers? — cheap for tooth and 'air brush, vests, night-shirt, stockings, and sundries.

"Make the best of it," and presently, when it came to hair-brushing, he had to smooth his troubled locks with his hands. It was a poor result. "Sneak out and get a shave, I suppose, and buy a brush and so on. Chink again! Beard don't show much."

He ran his hand over his chin, looked at himself steadfastly for some time, and curled his insufficient moustache up with some care. Then he fell a-meditating on his beauty. He considered himself, three-quarter face, left and right. An expression of distaste crept over his features. " Looking won't alter it, Hoopdriver," he remarked. " You're a weedy customer, my man. Shoulders narrow. Skimpy, anyhow."

He put his knuckles on the toilet table and regarded himself with his chin lifted in the air. " Good Lord!" he said. "*What* a neck! Wonder why I got such a thundering lump there."

He sat down on the bed, his eye still on the glass. " If I'd been exercised properly, if I'd been fed reasonable, if I hadn't been shoved out of a silly school into a silly shop — But there! the old folks didn't know no better. The schoolmaster ought to have. But he didn't, poor old fool! — Still, when it comes to meeting a girl like this — It's '*ard*.

" I wonder what Adam 'd think of me — as a specimen. Civilisation, eigh? Heir of the ages! I'm nothing. I know nothing. I can't do anything — sketch a bit. Why wasn't I made an artist?

" Beastly cheap, after all, this suit does look, in the sunshine."

"No good, Hoopdriver. Anyhow, you don't tell yourself any lies about it. Lovers ain't your game, — anyway. But there's other things yet. You can help the young lady, and you will — I suppose she'll be going home — And that business of the bicycle's to see to, too, my man. *Forward*, Hoopdriver! If you ain't a beauty, that's no reason why you should stop and be copped, is it?"

And having got back in this way to a gloomy kind of self-satisfaction, he had another attempt at his hair preparatory to leaving his room and hurrying on breakfast, for an early departure. While breakfast was preparing he wandered out into South Street and refurnished himself with the elements of luggage again. "No expense to be spared," he murmured, disgorging the half-sovereign.

THE DEPARTURE FROM CHICHESTER

XXVIII

He caused his 'sister' to be called repeatedly, and when she came down, explained with a humorous smile his legal relationship to the bicycle in the yard. "Might be disagreeable, y' know." His anxiety was obvious enough. "Very well," she said (quite friendly); "hurry breakfast, and we'll ride out. I want to talk things over with you." The girl seemed more beautiful than ever after the night's sleep; her hair in comely dark waves from her forehead, her ungauntleted finger-tips pink and cool. And how decided she was! Breakfast was a nervous ceremony, conversation fraternal but thin; the waiter overawed him, and he was cowed by a multiplicity of forks. But she called him "Chris." They discussed their route over his sixpenny county map for the sake of talking, but avoided a decision in the presence of the attendant. The five-pound note was changed for the bill, and through Hoopdriver's determination to be quite the gentleman, the waiter and chambermaid got half a crown each and the ostler a florin. "'Olidays," said the ostler to himself, without gratitude. The public mounting of the bicycles in the street was a moment of trepidation. A policeman actually stopped and watched them from the opposite kerb. Suppose him to come across and ask: "Is that your bicycle, sir?" Fight? Or drop it and run? It was a time of bewildering apprehension, too, going through the streets of the town, so that a milk cart barely escaped destruction under Mr. Hoopdriver's chancy wheel. That recalled him to a sense of erratic steering, and he pulled himself together. In the lanes he breathed freer, and a less formal conversation presently began.

"You've ridden out of Chichester in a great hurry," said Jessie.

"Well, the fact of it is, I'm worried, just a little bit. About this machine."

"Of course," she said. "I had forgotten that. But where are we going?"

"Jest a turning or two more, if you don't mind," said Hoopdriver. "Jest a mile or so. I have to think of you, you know. I should feel more easy. If we was locked up, you know — Not that I should mind on my own account —"

They rode with a streaky, grey sea coming and going on their left hand. Every mile they put between themselves and Chichester Mr. Hoopdriver felt a little less conscience-stricken, and a little more of the gallant desperado. Here he was riding on a splendid machine with a Slap-up girl beside him. What would they think of it in the Emporium if any of them were to see him? He imagined in detail the astonishment of Miss Isaacs and of Miss Howe. "Why! It's Mr. Hoopdriver," Miss Isaacs would say. "*Never!*" emphatically from Miss Howe. Then he played with Briggs, and then tried the 'G. V.' in a shay. " Fancy introjuicing 'em to her — My sister *pro tem.*" He was her brother Chris — Chris what? — Confound it! Harringon, Hartington — something like that. Have to keep off that topic until he could remember. Wish he'd told her the truth now — almost. He glanced at her. She was riding with her eyes straight ahead of her. Thinking. A little perplexed, perhaps, she seemed. He noticed how well she rode and that she rode with her lips closed — a thing he could never manage.

Mr. Hoopdriver's mind came round to the future. What was she going to do? What were they both going to do? His thoughts took a graver colour. He had rescued her. This was fine, manly rescue work he was engaged upon. She ought to go home, in spite of that stepmother. He must insist gravely but firmly upon that. She was the spirited sort, of course, but still — Wonder if she had any money? Wonder what the second-class fare from Havant to London is? Of course he would have to pay that — it was the regular thing, he being a gentleman. Then should he take her home? He began to rough in a moving sketch of the return. The stepmother, repentant of her indescribable cruelties, would be present, — even these rich people have their troubles, — probably an uncle or two. The footman would announce, Mr. — (bother that name!) and Miss Milton. Then two women weeping together, and a knightly figure in the background dressed in a handsome Norfolk jacket, still conspicuously new. He would conceal his feeling until the very end. Then, leaving, he would pause in the doorway in such an attitude as Mr. George Alexander might assume, and say, slowly and dwindlingly: "Be kind to her — *be* kind to her," and so depart, heartbroken to the meanest intelligence. But that was a matter for the future. He would have to begin discussing the return soon. There was no traffic along the road, and he came up beside her (he had fallen behind in his musing). She began to talk. "Mr. Denison," she began, and then, doubtfully, "That *is* your name? I'm very stupid — "

"It is," said Mr. Hoopdriver. (Denison, was it? Denison, Denison, Denison. What was she saying?)

"I wonder how far you are willing to help me?"

Confoundedly hard to answer a question like that on the spur of the moment, without steering wildly. "You may rely — " said Mr. Hoopdriver, recovering from a violent wabble. "I can assure you — I want to help you very much. Don't consider me at all. Leastways, consider me entirely at your service." (Nuisance not to be able to say this kind of thing right.)

"You see, I am so awkwardly situated."

"If I can only help you — you will make me very happy — " There was a pause. Round a bend in the road they came upon a grassy space between hedge and road, set with yarrow and meadowsweet, where a felled tree lay among the green. There she dismounted, and propping her machine against a stone, sat down. "Here, we can talk," she said.

"Yes," said Mr. Hoopdriver, expectant.

She answered after a little while, sitting, elbow on knee, with her chin in her hand, and looking straight in front of her. "I don't know — I am resolved to Live my Own Life."

"Of course," said Mr. Hoopdriver. "Naturally."

"I want to Live, and I want to see what life means. I want to learn. Everyone is hurrying me, everything is hurrying me; I want time to think."

Mr. Hoopdriver was puzzled, but admiring. It

was wonderful how clear and ready her words were. But then one might well speak well with a throat and lips like that. He knew he was inadequate, but he tried to meet the occasion. "If you let them rush you into anything you might repent of, of course you'd be very silly," he said.

"Don't *you* want to learn?" she asked.

"I was wondering only this morning," he began, and stopped.

She was too intent upon her own thoughts to notice this insufficiency. "I find myself in life, and it terrifies me. I seem to be like a little speck whirling on a wheel, suddenly caught up. 'What am I here for?' I ask. Simply to be here a time — I asked it a week ago, I asked it yesterday, and I ask it to-day. And little things happen and the days pass. My stepmother takes me shopping, people come to tea, there is a new play to pass the time, or a concert, or a novel. The wheels of the world go on turning, turning. It is horrible. I want to do a miracle like Joshua and stop the whirl until I have fought it out. At home — It's impossible."

Mr. Hoopdriver stroked his moustache. "It *is* so," he said in a meditative tone. "Things *will* go on." The faint breath of summer stirred the trees, and a bunch of dandelion puff lifted among the meadowsweet and struck and broke into a dozen separate threads against his knee. They flew on apart, and sank, as the breeze fell, among the grass: some to germinate, some to perish. His eye followed them until they had vanished.

"I can't go back to Surbiton," said the Young Lady in Grey.

"*Eigh?*" said Mr. Hoopdriver, catching at his moustache. This was an unexpected development.

"I want to write, you see," said the Young Lady in Grey, "to write Books and alter things. To do Good. I want to lead a Free Life and Own myself. I can't go back. I want to obtain a position as a Journalist. I have been told — But I know no one to help me at once. No one that I could go to. There is one person — She was a mistress at my school. If I could write to her — But then, how could I get her answer?"

"H'mp," said Mr. Hoopdriver, very grave.

"I can't trouble you much more. You have come — you have risked things — "

"That don't count," said Mr. Hoopdriver. "It's double pay to let me do it, so to speak."

"It is good of you to say that. Surbiton is so Conventional. I am resolved to be Unconventional — at any cost. But we are so hampered. If I could only burgeon out of all that hinders me! I want to struggle, to take my place in the world. I want to be my own mistress, to shape my own career. But my stepmother objects so. She does as she likes herself, and is strict with me to ease her conscience. And if I go back now, go back owning myself beaten—" She left the rest to his imagination.

"I see that," agreed Mr. Hoopdriver. He *must* help her. Within his skull he was doing some intricate arithmetic with five pounds six and twopence. In some vague way he inferred from all this that Jessie was trying to escape from an undesirable marriage, but was saying these things out of modesty. His circle of ideas was so limited.

"You know, Mr.—I've forgotten your name again."

Mr. Hoopdriver seemed lost in abstraction. "You can't go back of course, quite like that," he said thoughtfully. His ears were suddenly red and his cheeks flushed.

"But what *is* your name?"

"Name!" said Mr. Hoopdriver. "Why!—Benson, of course."

"Mr. Benson—yes—it's really very stupid of me. But I can never remember names. I must make a note on my cuff." She clicked a little silver pencil and wrote the name down. "If I could write to my friend. I believe she would be able to help me to an independent life. I could write to her—

or telegraph. Write, I think. I could scarcely explain in a telegram. I know she would help me."

Clearly there was only one course open to a gentleman under the circumstances. "In that case," said Mr. Hoopdriver, "if you don't mind trusting yourself to a stranger, we might continue as we are perhaps. For a day or so. Until you heard." (Suppose thirty shillings a day, that gives four days, say four thirties is hun' and twenty, six quid, — well, three days, say; four ten.)

"You are very good to me."

His expression was eloquent.

"Very well, then, and thank you. It's wonderful — it's more than I deserve that you — " She dropped the theme abruptly. "What was our bill at Chichester?"

"Eigh?" said Mr. Hoopdriver, feigning a certain stupidity. There was a brief discussion. Secretly he was delighted at her insistence in paying. She carried her point. Their talk came round to their immediate plans for the day. They decided to ride easily, through Havant, and stop, perhaps, at Fareham or Southampton. For the previous day had tried them both. Holding the map extended on his knee, Mr. Hoopdriver's eye fell by chance on the bicycle at his feet. "That bicycle," he remarked, quite irrelevantly, "wouldn't look the same machine if I got a big, double Elarum instead of that little bell."

"Why?"

"Jest a thought." A pause.

"Very well, then, — Havant and lunch," said Jessie, rising.

"I wish, somehow, we could have managed it without stealing that machine," said Hoopdriver. "Because it *is* stealing it, you know, come to think of it."

"Nonsense. If Mr. Bechamel troubles you — I will tell the whole world — if need be."

"I believe you would," said Mr. Hoopdriver, admiring her. "You're plucky enough — goodness knows."

Discovering suddenly that she was standing, he, too, rose and picked up her machine. She took it and wheeled it into the road. Then he took his own. He paused, regarding it. "I say!" said he. "How'd this bike look, now, if it was enamelled grey?"

She looked over her shoulder at his grave face. "Why try and hide it in that way?"

"It was jest a passing thought," said Mr. Hoopdriver, airily. "Didn't *mean* anything, you know."

As they were riding on to Havant it occurred to Mr. Hoopdriver in a transitory manner that the interview had been quite other than his expectation.

But that was the way with everything in Mr. Hoopdriver's experience. And though his Wisdom looked grave within him, and Caution was chinking coins, and an ancient prejudice in favour of Property shook her head, something else was there too, shouting in his mind to drown all these saner considerations, the intoxicating thought of riding beside Her all to-day, all to-morrow, perhaps for other days after that. Of talking to her familiarly, being brother of all her slender strength and freshness, of having a golden, real, and wonderful time beyond all his imaginings. His old familiar fancyings gave place to anticipations as impalpable and fluctuating and beautiful as the sunset of a summer day.

At Havant he took an opportunity to purchase, at a small hairdresser's in the main street, a toothbrush, a pair of nail scissors, and a little bottle of stuff to darken the moustache, an article the shopman introduced to his attention, recommended highly, and sold in the excitement of the occasion.

THE UNEXPECTED ANECDOTE OF THE LION

XXIX

THEY rode on to Cosham and lunched lightly but expensively there. Jessie went out and posted her letter to her school friend. Then the green height of Portsdown Hill tempted them, and leaving their machines in the village they clambered up the slope to the silent red-brick fort that crowned it. Thence they had a view of Portsmouth and its cluster of sister towns, the crowded narrows of the harbour, the Solent and the Isle of Wight like a blue cloud through the hot haze. Jessie by some miracle had become a skirted woman in the Cosham inn. Mr. Hoopdriver lounged gracefully on the turf, smoked a Red Herring cigarette, and lazily regarded the fortified towns that spread like a map away there, the inner line of defence like toy fortifications, a mile off perhaps; and beyond that a few little fields and then the beginnings of Landport suburb and the smoky cluster of the multitudinous houses. To the right at the head of the harbour shallows the town of Porchester rose among the trees. Mr. Hoopdriver's anxiety receded to some remote corner of his brain and that florid half-voluntary imagination of his shared the stage with the image of Jessie. He began to speculate on the impression he was creating. He took stock of his suit in a more optimistic spirit, and reviewed, with some complacency, his actions for the last four and twenty hours. Then he was dashed at the thought of her infinite perfections.

She had been observing him quietly, rather more closely during the last hour or so. She did not look at him directly because he seemed always looking at her. Her own troubles had quieted down a little, and her curiosity about the chivalrous, worshipping, but singular gentleman in brown, was awakening. She had recalled, too, the curious incident of their first encounter. She found him hard to explain to herself. You must understand that her knowledge of the world was rather less than nothing, having been obtained entirely from books. You must not take a certain ignorance for foolishness.

She had begun with a few experiments. He did not know French except '*sivverplay,*' a phrase he seemed to regard as a very good light table joke in itself. His English was uncertain, but not such as books informed her distinguished the lower classes.

His manners seemed to her good on the whole, but a trifle over-respectful and out of fashion. He called her 'Madam' once. He seemed a person of means and leisure, but he knew nothing of recent concerts, theatres, or books. How did he spend his time? He was certainly chivalrous, and a trifle simple-minded. She fancied (so much is there in a change of costume) that she had never met with such a man before. What *could* he be?

"Mr. Benson," she said, breaking a silence devoted to landscape.

He rolled over and regarded her, chin on knuckles.

"At your service."

"Do you paint? Are you an artist?"

"Well." Judicious pause. "I should hardly call myself a Nartist, you know. I *do* paint a little. And sketch, you know — skitty kind of things."

He plucked and began to nibble a blade of grass. It was really not so much lying as his quick imagination that prompted him to add, "In Papers, you know, and all that."

"I see," said Jessie, looking at him thoughtfully. Artists were a very heterogeneous class certainly, and geniuses had a trick of being a little odd. He avoided her eye and bit his grass. "I don't do *much*, you know."

"It's not your profession?"

"Oh, no," said Hoopdriver, anxious now to hedge. "I don't make a regular thing of it, you know. Jest now and then something comes into my head and down it goes. No — I'm not a *regular* artist."

"Then you don't practise any regular profession?"

Mr. Hoopdriver looked into her eyes and saw their quiet unsuspicious regard. He had vague ideas of resuming the detective *rôle*. "It's like this," he said, to gain time. "I have a sort of profession. Only there's a kind of reason — nothing much, you know — "

"I beg your pardon for cross-examining you."

"No trouble," said Mr. Hoopdriver. "Only I can't very well — I leave it to you, you know. I don't want to make any mystery of it, so far as that goes." Should he plunge boldly and be a barrister? That anyhow was something pretty good. But she might know about barristry.

"I think I could guess what you are."

"Well — guess," said Mr. Hoopdriver.

"You come from one of the colonies?'

"Dear me!" said Mr. Hoopdriver, veering round to the new wind. "How did you find out *that?*" (the man was born in a London suburb, dear Reader.)

"I guessed," she said.

He lifted his eyebrows as one astonished, and clutched a new piece of grass.

"You were educated up country."

"Good again," said Hoopdriver, rolling over again into her elbow. "You're a *clairvoy* ant." He bit at the grass, smiling. "Which colony was it?"

"That I don't know."

"You must guess," said Hoopdriver.

"South Africa," she said. "I strongly incline to South Africa."

"South Africa's quite a large place," he said.

"But South Africa is right?"

"You're warm," said Hoopdriver, "anyhow," and the while his imagination was eagerly exploring this new province.

"South Africa *is* right?" she insisted.

He turned over again and nodded, smiling reassuringly into her eyes.

"What made me think of South Africa was that novel of Olive Schreiner's, you know — 'The Story of an African Farm.' Gregory Rose is so like you."

"I never read 'The Story of an African Farm,'" said Hoopdriver. "I must. What's he like?"

"You must read the book. But it's a wonderful place, with its mixture of races, and its brand-new civilisation jostling the old savagery. Were you near Khama?"

"He was a long way off from our place," said Mr. Hoopdriver. "We had a little ostrich farm, you know — Just a few hundred of 'em, out Johannesburg way."

"On the Karroo — was it called?"

"That's the term. Some of it was freehold though. Luckily. We got along very well in the old days. — But there's no ostriches on that farm now." He had a diamond mine in his head, just at the moment, but he stopped and left a little to the girl's imagination. Besides which it had occurred to him with a kind of shock that he was lying.

"What became of the ostriches?"

"We sold 'em off, when we parted with the farm. Do you mind if I have another cigarette? That was when I was quite a little chap, you know, that we had this ostrich farm."

"Did you have Blacks and Boers about you?"

"Lots," said Mr. Hoopdriver, striking a match on his instep and beginning to feel hot at the new responsibility he had brought upon himself.

"How interesting! Do you know, I've never been out of England except to Paris and Mentone and Switzerland."

"One gets tired of travelling (*puff*) after a bit, of course."

"You must tell me about your farm in South Africa. It always stimulates my imagination to think of these places. I can fancy all the tall ostriches being driven out by a black herd to — graze, I suppose. How do ostriches feed?"

"Well," said Hoopdriver. "That's rather various. They have their fancies, you know. There's fruit, of course, and that kind of thing. And chicken food, and so forth. You have to use judgment."

"Did you ever see a lion?"

"They weren't very common in our district," said Hoopdriver, quite modestly. "But I've seen them, of course. Once or twice."

"Fancy seeing a lion! Weren't you frightened?"

Mr. Hoopdriver was now thoroughly sorry he had accepted that offer of South Africa. He puffed his cigarette and regarded the Solent languidly as he settled the fate on that lion in his mind. "I scarcely had time," he said. "It all happened in a minute."

"Go on," she said.

"I was going across the inner paddock where the fatted ostriches were."

"Did you *eat* ostriches, then? I did not know—"

"Eat them!—often. Very nice they *are* too, properly stuffed. Well, we—I, rather—was going across this paddock, and I saw something standing up in the moonlight and looking at me." Mr. Hoopdriver was in a hot perspiration now. His invention seemed to have gone limp. "Luckily I had my father's gun with me. I *was* scared, though, I

can tell you. (*Puff.*) I just aimed at the end that I thought was the head. And let fly. (*Puff.*) And over it went, you know."

"Dead?"

"*As* dead. It was one of the luckiest shots I ever fired. And I wasn't much over nine at the time, neither."

"*I* should have screamed and run away."

"There's some things you can't run away from," said Mr. Hoopdriver. "To run would have been Death."

"I don't think I ever met a lion-killer before," she remarked, evidently with a heightened opinion of him.

There was a pause. She seemed meditating further questions. Mr. Hoopdriver drew his watch hastily. "I say," said Mr. Hoopdriver, showing it to her, "don't you think we ought to be getting on?"

His face was flushed, his ears bright red. She ascribed his confusion to modesty. He rose with a lion added to the burthens of his conscience, and held out his hand to assist her. They walked down into Cosham again, resumed their machines, and went on at a leisurely pace along the northern shore of the big harbour. But Mr. Hoopdriver was no longer happy. This horrible, this fulsome lie, stuck in his memory. Why *had* he done it? She did not ask for any more

South African stories, happily — at least until Porchester was reached — but talked instead of Living One's Own Life, and how custom hung on people like chains. She talked wonderfully, and set Hoopdriver's mind fermenting. By the Castle, Mr. Hoopdriver caught several crabs in little shore pools. At Fareham they stopped for a second tea, and left the place towards the hour of sunset, under such invigorating circumstances as you shall in due course hear.

THE RESCUE EXPEDITION

XXX

AND now to tell of those energetic chevaliers, Widgery, Dangle, and Phipps, and of that distressed beauty, 'Thomas Plantagenet,' well known in society, so the paragraphs said, as Mrs. Milton. We left them at Midhurst station, if I remember rightly, waiting, in a state of fine emotion, for the Chichester train. It was clearly understood by the entire Rescue Party that Mrs. Milton was bearing up bravely against almost overwhelming grief. The three gentlemen outdid one another in sympathetic expedients; they watched her gravely — almost tenderly. The substantial Widgery tugged at his moustache, and looked his unspeakable feelings at her with those dog-like, brown eyes of his; the slender Dangle tugged at *his* moustache, and did what he could with unsympathetic grey ones. Phipps, unhappily, had no moustache to run any risks with, so he folded his arms and talked in a brave, indifferent, bearing-up tone about the London, Brighton, and South Coast

Railway, just to cheer the poor woman up a little. And even Mrs. Milton really felt that exalted melancholy to the very bottom of her heart, and tried to show it in a dozen little, delicate, feminine ways.

"There is nothing to do until we get to Chichester," said Dangle. "Nothing."

"Nothing," said Widgery, and aside in her ear: "You really ate scarcely anything, you know."

"Their trains are always late," said Phipps, with his fingers along the edge of his collar.

Dangle, you must understand, was a sub-editor and reviewer, and his pride was to be Thomas Plantagenet's intellectual companion. Widgery, the big man, was manager of a bank and a mighty golfer, and his conception of his relations to her never came into his mind without those charming old lines, "Douglas, Douglas, tender and true," falling hard upon its heels. His name was Douglas — Douglas Widgery. And Phipps, Phipps was a medical student still, and he felt that he laid his heart at her feet, the heart of a man of the world. She was kind to them all in her way, and insisted on their being friends together, in spite of a disposition to reciprocal criticism they displayed. Dangle thought Widgery a Philistine, appreciating but coarsely the merits of "A Soul Untrammelled," and Widgery thought Dangle lacked humanity — would talk insincerely to say a clever thing. Both Dangle and Widgery thought Phipps a bit of a cub, and Phipps thought both Dangle and Widgery a couple of Thundering Bounders.

"They would have got to Chichester in time for lunch," said Dangle, in the train. "After, perhaps. And there's no sufficient place in the road. So soon as we get there, Phipps must inquire at the chief hotels to see if any one answering to her description has lunched there."

"Oh, *I'll* inquire," said Phipps. "Willingly. I suppose you and Widgery will just hang about — "

He saw an expression of pain on Mrs. Milton's gentle face, and stopped abruptly.

"No," said Dangle, "we shan't *hang about*, as you put it. There are two places in Chichester where tourists might go — the cathedral and a remarkably fine museum. I shall go to the cathedral and make an inquiry or so, while Widgery — "

"The museum. Very well. And after that there's a little thing or two I've thought of myself," said Widgery.

To begin with they took Mrs. Milton in a kind of procession to the Red Hotel and established her there with some tea. "You are so kind to me," she said. "All of you." They signified that it was nothing, and dispersed to their inquiries. By six they returned, their zeal a little damped, without news. Widgery came back with Dangle. Phipps was the last to return. "You're quite sure," said Widgery, "that there isn't any flaw in that inference of yours?"

"Quite," said Dangle, rather shortly.

"Of course," said Widgery, "their starting from Midhurst on the Chichester road doesn't absolutely bind them not to change their minds."

"My dear fellow! It does. Really it does. You must allow me to have enough intelligence to think of cross-roads. Really you must. There aren't any cross-roads to tempt them. Would they turn aside here? No. Would they turn there? Many more things are inevitable than you fancy."

"We shall see at once," said Widgery, at the window. "Here comes Phipps. For my own part—"

"Phipps!" said Mrs. Milton. "Is he hurrying? Does he look—" She rose in her eagerness, biting her trembling lip, and went towards the window.

"No news," said Phipps, entering.

"Ah!" said Widgery.

"None?" said Dangle.

"Well," said Phipps. "One fellow had got hold of a queer story of a man in bicycling clothes, who was asking the same question about this time yesterday."

"What question?" said Mrs. Milton, in the

shadow of the window. She spoke in a low voice, almost a whisper.

"Why — Have you seen a young lady in a grey bicycling costume?"

Dangle caught at his lower lip. "What's that?" he said. "Yesterday! A man asking after her then! What can *that* mean?"

"Heaven knows," said Phipps, sitting down wearily. "You'd better infer."

"What kind of man?" said Dangle.

"How should I know? — in bicycling costume, the fellow said."

"But what height? — What complexion?"

"Didn't ask," said Phipps.

"*Didn't ask!* Nonsense," said Dangle.

"Ask him yourself," said Phipps. "He's an ostler chap in the White Hart, — short, thick-set fellow, with a red face and a crusty manner. Leaning up against the stable door. Smells of whiskey. Go and ask him."

"Of course," said Dangle, taking his straw hat from the shade over the stuffed bird on the chiffonier and turning towards the door. "I might have known."

Phipps' mouth opened and shut.

"You're tired, I'm sure, Mr. Phipps," said the lady, soothingly. "Let me ring for some tea for you." It suddenly occurred to Phipps that he had lapsed a little from his chivalry. "I was a little annoyed at the way he rushed me to do all this business," he said. "But I'd do a hundred times as much if it would bring *you* any nearer to her." Pause. "I *would* like a little tea."

"I don't want to raise any false hopes," said Widgery. "But I do *not* believe they even came to Chichester. Dangle's a very clever fellow, of course, but sometimes these Inferences of his—"

"Tchak!" said Phipps, suddenly.

"What is it?" said Mrs. Milton.

"Something I've forgotten. I went right out from here, went to every other hotel in the place, and never thought—But never mind. I'll ask when the waiter comes."

"You don't mean—"

A tap, and the door opened. "Tea, m'm? yes, m'm," said the waiter.

"One minute," said Phipps. "Was a lady in grey, a cycling lady—"

"Stopped here yesterday? Yessir. Stopped the night. With her brother, sir—a young gent."

"Brother!" said Mrs. Milton, in a low tone. "Thank God!"

The waiter glanced at her and understood everything. "A young gent, sir," he said, "very free with his money. Give the name of Beaumont."

He proceeded to some rambling particulars, and was cross-examined by Widgery on the plans of the young couple.

"Havant! Where's Havant?" said Phipps. "I seem to remember it somewhere."

"Was the man tall?" said Mrs. Milton, intently, "distinguished looking? with a long, flaxen moustache? and spoke with a drawl?"

"Well," said the waiter, and thought. "His moustache, m'm, was scarcely long — scrubby more, and young looking."

"About thirty-five, he was?"

"No, m'm. More like five and twenty. Not that."

"Dear me!" said Mrs. Milton, speaking in a curious, hollow voice, fumbling for her salts, and showing the finest self-control. "It must have been her *younger* brother — must have been."

"That will do, thank you," said Widgery, officiously, feeling that she would be easier under this new surprise if the man were dismissed. The waiter turned to go, and almost collided with Dangle, who was entering the room, panting excitedly and with a pocket handkerchief held to his right eye. "Hullo!" said Dangle. "What's up?"

"What's up with *you?*" said Phipps.

"Nothing — an altercation merely with that

drunken ostler of yours. He thought it was a plot to annoy him — that the Young Lady in Grey was mythical. Judged from your manner. I've got a piece of raw meat to keep over it. You have some news, I see?"

"Did the man hit you?" asked Widgery.

Mrs. Milton rose and approached Dangle. "Cannot I do anything?"

Dangle was heroic. "Only tell me your news," he said, round the corner of the handkerchief.

"It was in this way," said Phipps, and explained rather sheepishly. While he was doing so, with a running fire of commentary from Widgery, the waiter brought in a tray of tea. "A time table," said Dangle, promptly, "for Havant." Mrs. Milton poured two cups, and Phipps and Dangle partook in passover form. They caught the train by a hair's breadth. So to Havant and inquiries.

Dangle was puffed up to find that his guess of Havant was right. In view of the fact that beyond Havant the Southampton road has a steep hill continuously on the right-hand side, and the sea on the left, he hit upon a magnificent scheme for heading the young folks off. He and Mrs. Milton would go to Fareham, Widgery and Phipps should alight one each at the intermediate stations of Cosham and Porchester, and come on by the next train if they had no news. If they did not come on, a wire to the Fareham post office was to explain why. It was Napoleonic, and more than consoled Dangle for the open derision of the Havant street boys at the handkerchief which still protected his damaged eye.

Moreover, the scheme answered to perfection. The fugitives escaped by a hair's breadth. They were outside the Golden Anchor at Fareham, and preparing to mount, as Mrs. Milton and Dangle came round the corner from the station. "It's her!" said Mrs. Milton, and would have screamed. "Hist!" said Dangle, gripping the lady's arm, removing his handkerchief in his excitement, and leaving the piece of meat over his eye, an extraordinary appearance which seemed unexpectedly to calm her. "Be cool!" said Dangle, glaring under the meat. "They must not see us. They will get away else. Were there flys at the station?" The young couple mounted and vanished round the corner of the Winchester road. Had it not been for the publicity of the business, Mrs. Milton would have fainted. "*Save her!*" she said.

"Ah! A conveyance," said Dangle. "One minute."

He left her in a most pathetic attitude, with her hand pressed to her heart, and rushed into the Golden Anchor. Dog cart in ten minutes.

Emerged. The meat had gone now, and one saw the cooling puffiness over his eye. "I will conduct you back to the station," said Dangle; "hurry back here, and pursue them. You will meet Widgery and Phipps and tell them I am in pursuit."

She was whirled back to the railway station and left there, on a hard, blistered, wooden seat in the sun. She felt tired and dreadfully ruffled and agitated and dusty. Dangle was, no doubt, most energetic and devoted; but for a kindly, helpful manner commend her to Douglas Widgery.

Meanwhile Dangle, his face golden in the evening sun, was driving (as well as he could) a large, black horse harnessed into a thing called a gig, north-westward towards Winchester. Dangle, barring his swollen eye, was a refined-looking little man, and he wore a deerstalker cap and was dressed in dark grey. His neck was long and slender. Perhaps you know what gigs are, — huge, big, wooden things and very high; and the horse, too, was huge and big and high, with knobby legs, a long face, a hard mouth, and a whacking trick of pacing. Smack, smack, smack, smack it went along the road, and hard by the church it shied vigorously at a hooded perambulator.

The history of the Rescue Expedition now becomes confused. It appears that Widgery was extremely indignant to find Mrs. Milton left about upon the Fareham platform. The day had irritated him somehow, though he had started with the noblest intentions, and he seemed glad to find an outlet for justifiable indignation. "He's such a spasmodic creature," said Widgery. "Rushing off! And I suppose we're to wait here until he comes back! It's likely. He's so egotistical, is Dangle. Always wants to mismanage everything himself."

"He means to help me," said Mrs. Milton, a little reproachfully, touching his arm.

Widgery was hardly in the mood to be mollified all at once. "He need not prevent *me*," he said, and stopped. "It's no good talking, you know, and you are tired."

"I can go on," she said brightly; "if only we find her."

"While I was cooling my heels in Cosham I bought a county map." He produced and opened it. "Here, you see, is the road out of Fareham." He proceeded with the calm deliberation of a business man to develop a proposal of taking train forthwith to Winchester. "They *must* be going to Winchester," he explained. It was inevitable. To-morrow Sunday, Winchester a cathedral town, road going nowhere else of the slightest importance.

"But Mr. Dangle?"

"He will simply go on until he has to pass something, and then he will break his neck. I have seen Dangle drive before. It's scarcely likely a dog-cart, especially a hired dog-cart, will overtake bicycles in the cool of the evening. Rely upon me, Mrs. Milton—"

"I am in your hands," she said, with pathetic littleness, looking up at him, and for the moment he forgot the exasperation of the day.

Phipps, during this conversation, had stood in a somewhat depressed attitude, leaning on his stick, feeling his collar, and looking from one speaker to the other. The idea of leaving Dangle behind seemed to him an excellent one. "We might leave a message at the place where he got the dog-cart," he suggested, when he saw their eyes meeting. There was a cheerful alacrity about all three at the proposal.

But they never got beyond Botley. For even as their train ran into the station, a mighty rumbling was heard, there was a shouting overhead, the guard stood astonished on the platform, and Phipps, thrusting his head out of the window, cried, "There he goes!" and sprang out of the carriage. Mrs. Milton, following in alarm, just saw it. From Widgery it was hidden. Botley station lies in a cutting, overhead was the roadway, and across the lemon yellows

and flushed pinks of the sunset, there whirled a great black mass, a horse like a long-nosed chess knight, the upper works of a gig, and Dangle in transit from front to back. A monstrous shadow aped him across the cutting. It was the event of a second. Dangle seemed to jump, hang in the air momentarily, and vanish, and after a moment's pause came a heart-rending smash. Then two black heads running swiftly.

"Better get out," said Phipps to Mrs. Milton, who stood fascinated in the doorway.

In another moment all three were hurrying up the steps. They found Dangle, hatless, standing up with cut hands extended, having his hands brushed by an officious small boy. A broad, ugly road ran downhill in a long vista, and in the distance was a little group of Botley inhabitants holding the big, black horse. Even at that distance they could see the expression of conscious pride on the monster's visage. It was as wooden-faced a horse as you can imagine. The beasts in the Tower of London, on which the men in armour are perched, are the only horses I have ever seen at all like it. However, we are not concerned now with the horse, but with Dangle. "Hurt?" asked Phipps, eagerly, leading.

"Mr. Dangle!" cried Mrs. Milton, clasping her hands.

"Hullo!" said Dangle, not surprised in the slightest. "Glad you've come. I may want you. Bit of a mess I'm in — eigh? But I've caught 'em. At the very place I expected, too."

"Caught them!" said Widgery. "Where are they?"

"Up there," he said, with a backward motion of his head. "About a mile up the hill. I left 'em. I *had* to."

"I don't understand," said Mrs. Milton, with that rapt, painful look again. "Have you found Jessie?"

"I have. I wish I could wash the gravel out of my hands somewhere. It was like this, you know. Came on them suddenly round a corner. Horse shied at the bicycles. They were sitting by the roadside botanising flowers. I just had time to shout, 'Jessie Milton, we've been looking for you,' and then that confounded brute bolted. I didn't dare turn round. I had all my work to do to save myself being turned over, as it was — so long as I did, I mean. I just shouted, 'Return to your friends. All will be forgiven.' And off I came, clatter, clatter. Whether they heard — "

"*Take me to her*," said Mrs. Milton, with intensity, turning towards Widgery.

"Certainly," said Widgery, suddenly becoming active. "How far is it, Dangle?"

"Mile and a half or two miles. I was determined to find them, you know. I say though — Look at my hands! But I beg your pardon, Mrs. Milton." He turned to Phipps. "Phipps, I say, where shall I wash the gravel out? And have a look at my knee?"

"There's the station," said Phipps, becoming helpful. Dangle made a step, and a damaged knee became evident. "Take my arm," said Phipps.

"Where can we get a conveyance?" asked Widgery of two small boys.

The two small boys failed to understand. They looked at one another.

"There's not a cab, not a go-cart, in sight," said Widgery. "It's a case of a horse, a horse, my kingdom for a horse."

"There's a harse all right," said one of the small boys with a movement of the head.

"Don't you know where we can hire traps?" asked Widgery.

"Or a cart or — anything?" asked Mrs. Milton.

"John Ooker's gart a cart, but no one can't 'ire'n," said the larger of the small boys, partially averting his face and staring down the road and making a song of it. "And so's my feyther, for's leg us broke."

"Not a cart even! Evidently. What shall we do?"

It occurred to Mrs. Milton that if Widgery was the man for courtly devotion, Dangle was infinitely readier of resource. "I suppose —" she said, timidly. "Perhaps if you were to ask Mr. Dangle —"

And then all the gilt came off Widgery. He answered quite rudely. "Confound Dangle! Hasn't he messed us up enough? He must needs drive after them in a trap to tell them we're coming, and now you want me to ask him —"

Her beautiful blue eyes were filled with tears. He stopped abruptly. "I'll go and ask Dangle," he said, shortly. "If you wish it." And went striding into the station and down the steps, leaving her in the road under the quiet inspection of the two little boys, and with a kind of ballad refrain running through her head, "Where are the Knights of the Olden Time?" and feeling tired to death and hungry and dusty and out of curl, and, in short, a martyr woman.

XXXI

It goes to my heart to tell of the end of that day, how the fugitives vanished into Immensity; how there were no more trains ; how Botley stared unsympathetically with a palpable disposition to derision, denying conveyances; how the landlord of the Heron was suspicious, how the next day was Sunday, and the hot summer's day had crumpled the collar of Phipps and stained the skirts of Mrs. Milton, and dimmed the radiant emotions of the whole party. Dangle, with sticking-plaster and a black eye, felt the absurdity of the pose of the Wounded Knight, and abandoned it after the faintest efforts. Recriminations never, perhaps, held the foreground of the talk, but they played like summer lightning on the edge of the conversation. And deep in the hearts of all was a galling sense of the ridiculous. Jessie, they thought, was most to blame. Apparently, too, the worst, which would have made the whole business tragic, was not happening. Here was a young woman — young woman do I say ? a mere girl! — had chosen to leave a comfortable home in Surbiton, and all the delights of a refined and intellectual circle, and had rushed off, trailing us after her, posing hard, mutually jealous, and now tired and weather-worn, to flick us off at last, mere mud from her wheel, into this detestable village beer-house on a Saturday night! And she had done it, not for Love and Passion, which are serious excuses one may recognise even if one must reprobate, but just for a Freak, just for a fantastic Idea; for nothing, in fact, but the outraging of Common Sense. Yet withal, such was our restraint, that we talked of her still as one much misguided, as one who burthened us with anxiety, as a lamb astray, and Mrs. Milton having eaten, continued to show the finest feelings on the matter.

She sat, I may mention, in the cushioned basket-chair, the only comfortable chair in the room, and we sat on incredibly hard, horsehair things having antimacassars tied to their backs by means of lemon-coloured bows. It was different from those dear old talks at Surbiton, somehow. She sat facing the window, which was open (the night was so tranquil and warm), and the dim light — for we did not use the lamp — suited her admirably. She talked in a voice that told you she was tired, and she seemed inclined to state a case against herself in the matter of "A Soul Untrammelled." It was such an evening as might live in a sympathetic memoir, but it was a little dull while it lasted.

"I feel," she said, "that I am to blame. I have Developed. That first book of mine — I do not go back upon a word of it, mind, but it has been misunderstood, misapplied."

"It has," said Widgery, trying to look so deeply sympathetic as to be visible in the dark. "Deliberately misunderstood."

"Don't say that," said the lady. "Not deliberately. I try and think that critics are honest. After their lights. I was not thinking of critics. But she, I mean — " She paused, an interrogation.

"It is possible," said Dangle, scrutinising his sticking-plaster.

"I write a book and state a case. I want people to *think* as I recommend, not to *do* as I recommend. It is just Teaching. Only I make it into a story. I want to Teach new Ideas, new Lessons, to promulgate Ideas. Then when the Ideas have been spread abroad — Things will come about. Only now it is madness to fly in the face of the established order. Bernard Shaw, you know, has explained that with regard to Socialism. We all know that to earn all you consume is right, and that living on invested capital is wrong. Only we cannot begin while we are so few. It is Those Others."

"Precisely," said Widgery. "It is Those Others. They must begin first."

"And meanwhile you go on banking—"

"If I didn't, some one else would."

"And I live on Mr. Milton's Lotion while I try to gain a footing in Literature."

"*Try!*" said Phipps. "You *have* done so." And, "That's different," said Dangle, at the same time.

"You are so kind to me. But in this matter. Of course Georgina Griffiths in my book lived alone in a flat in Paris and went to life classes and had men visitors, but then she was over twenty-one."

"Jessica is only seventeen, and girlish for that," said Dangle.

"It alters everything. That child! It is different with a woman. And Georgina Griffiths never flaunted her freedom—on a bicycle, in country places. In this country. Where every one is so particular. Fancy, *sleeping* away from home. It's dreadful— If it gets about it spells ruin for her."

"Ruin," said Widgery.

"No man would marry a girl like that," said Phipps.

"It must be hushed up," said Dangle.

"It always seems to me that life is made up of individuals, of individual cases. We must weigh each person against his or her circumstances. General rules don't apply—"

"I often feel the force of that," said Widgery.

"Those are my rules. Of course my books—"

"It's different, altogether different," said Dangle. "A novel deals with typical cases."

"And life is not typical," said Widgery, with immense profundity.

Then suddenly, unintentionally, being himself most surprised and shocked of any in the room, Phipps yawned. The failing was infectious, and the gathering having, as you can easily understand, talked itself weary, dispersed on trivial pretences. But not to sleep immediately. Directly Dangle was alone he began, with infinite disgust, to scrutinise his darkling eye, for he was a neat-minded little man in spite of his energy. The whole business— so near a capture—was horribly vexatious. Phipps sat on his bed for some time examining, with equal disgust, a collar he would have thought incredible for Sunday twenty-four hours before. Mrs. Milton fell a-musing on the mortality of even big, fat men with dog-like eyes, and Widgery was unhappy because he had been so cross to her at the station, and because so far he did not feel that he had scored over Dangle. Also he was angry with Dangle. And all four of them, being souls living very much upon the appearances of things, had a painful, mental middle distance of Botley derisive and suspicious, and a remoter background of London humorous, and Surbiton speculative. Were they really, after all, behaving absurdly?

MR. HOOPDRIVER, KNIGHT ERRANT

XXXII

As Mr. Dangle had witnessed, the fugitives had been left by him by the side of the road about two miles from Botley. Before Mr. Dangle's appearance, Mr. Hoopdriver had been learning with great interest that mere roadside flowers had names, — star-flowers, wind-stars, St. John's wort, willow herb, lords and ladies, bachelor's buttons, — most curious names, some of them. "The flowers are all different in South Africa, y'know," he was explaining with a happy fluke of his imagination to account for his ignorance. Then suddenly, heralded by clattering sounds and a gride of wheels, Dangle had flared and thundered across the tranquillity of the summer evening; Dangle, swaying and gesticulating behind a corybantic black horse, had hailed Jessie by her name, had backed towards the hedge for no ostensible reason, and vanished to the accomplishment of the Fate that had been written down for him from the very beginning of things. Jessie and Hoopdriver had scarcely time to stand up and seize

their machines, before this tumultuous, this swift and wonderful passing of Dangle was achieved. He went from side to side of the road,—worse even than the riding forth of Mr. Hoopdriver it was,—and vanished round the corner.

"He knew my name," said Jessie. "Yes—it was Mr. Dangle."

"That was our bicycles did that," said Mr. Hoopdriver simultaneously, and speaking with a certain complacent concern. "I hope he won't get hurt."

"That was Mr. Dangle," repeated Jessie, and Mr. Hoopdriver heard this time, with a violent start. His eyebrows went up spasmodically.

"What! someone you know?"

"Yes."

"Lord!"

"He was looking for me," said Jessie. "I could see. He began to call to me before the horse shied. My stepmother has sent him."

Mr. Hoopdriver wished he had returned the bicycle after all, for his ideas were still a little hazy about Bechamel and Mrs. Milton. Honesty *is* the best policy—often, he thought. He turned his head this way and that. He became active. "After us, eigh? Then he'll come back. He's gone down that hill, and he won't be able to pull up for a bit, I'm certain."

Jessie, he saw, had wheeled her machine into the road and was mounting. Still staring at the corner that had swallowed up Dangle, Hoopdriver followed suit. And so, just as the sun was setting, they began another flight together, — riding now towards Bishops Waltham, with Mr. Hoopdriver in the post of danger — the rear — ever and again looking over his shoulder and swerving dangerously as he did so. Occasionally Jessie had to slacken her pace. He breathed heavily, and hated himself because his mouth fell open. After nearly an hour's hard riding, they found themselves uncaught at Winchester. Not a trace of Dangle nor any other danger was visible as they rode into the dusky, yellow-lit street. Though the bats had been fluttering behind the hedges and the evening star was bright while they were still two miles from Winchester, Mr. Hoopdriver pointed out the dangers of stopping in such an obvious abiding-place, and gently but firmly insisted upon replenishing the lamps and riding on towards Salisbury. From Winchester, roads branch in every direction, and to turn abruptly westward was clearly the way to throw off the chase. As Hoopdriver saw the moon rising broad and yellow through the twilight, he thought he should revive the effect of that ride out of Bognor; but somehow, albeit the moon and all the atmospheric effects were the same, the emotions were different. They rode in absolute silence, and slowly after they had cleared the outskirts of Winchester. Both of them were now nearly tired out, — the level was tedious, and even a little hill a burden; and so it came about that in the hamlet of Wallenstock they were beguiled to stop and ask for accommodation in an exceptionally prosperous-looking village inn. A plausible landlady rose to the occasion.

Now, as they passed into the room where their suppers were prepared, Mr. Hoopdriver caught a glimpse through a door ajar and floating in a reek of smoke, of three and a half faces — for the edge of the door cut one down — and an American cloth-covered table with several glasses and a tankard. And he also heard a remark. In the second before he heard that remark, Mr. Hoopdriver had been a proud and happy man, — to particularize, a baronet's heir *incognito*. He had surrendered their bicycles to the odd man of the place with infinite easy dignity, and had bowingly opened the door for Jessie. "Who's that, then?" he imagined people saying; and then, "Some'n pretty well orf — judge by the bicycles." Then the imaginary spectators would fall a-talking of the fashionableness of bicycling, — how judges and stockbrokers and actresses and, in fact, all the best people rode, — and how that it was often the fancy of such great folk to shun the big hotels, the adulation of urban crowds, and seek, *incognito*, the cosy quaintnesses of village life. Then, maybe, they would think of a certain nameless air of distinction about the lady who had stepped across the doorway, and about the handsome, flaxen-moustached, blue-eyed Cavalier who had followed her in, and they would look one to another. "Tell you what it is," one of the village elders would say — just as they do in novels — voicing the thought of all, in a low, impressive tone: "There's such a thing as entertaining barranets unawares — not to mention no higher things — "

Such, I say, had been the filmy, delightful stuff in Mr. Hoopdriver's head the moment before he heard that remark. But the remark toppled him headlong. What the precise remark was need not concern us. It was a casual piece of such satire as Strephon delights in. Should you be curious, dear lady, as to its nature, you have merely to dress yourself in a really modern cycling costume, get one of the feeblest-looking of your men to escort you, and ride out, next Saturday evening, to any public house where healthy, homely people gather together. Then you will hear quite a lot of the kind of thing Mr. Hoopdriver heard. More, possibly, than you will desire.

The remark, I must add, implicated Mr. Hoopdriver. It indicated an entire disbelief in his social standing. At a blow, it shattered all the gorgeous imaginative fabric his mind had been rejoicing in. All that foolish happiness vanished like a dream. And there was nothing to show for it, as there is nothing to show for any spiteful remark that has ever been made. Perhaps the man who said the thing had a gleam of satisfaction at the idea of taking a complacent-looking fool down a peg, but it is just as possible he did not know at the time that his stray shot had hit. He had thrown it as a boy throws a stone at a bird. And it not only demolished a foolish, happy conceit, but it wounded. It touched Jessie grossly.

She did not hear it, he concluded from her subsequent bearing; but during the supper they had in the little private dining-room, though she talked cheerfully, he was preoccupied. Whiffs of indistinct conversation, and now and then laughter, came in from the inn parlour through the pelargoniums in the open window. Hoopdriver felt it must all be in the same strain,— at her expense and his. He answered her abstractedly. She was tired, she said, and presently went to her room. Mr. Hoopdriver, in his courtly way, opened the door for her and bowed her out. He stood listening and fearing some new offence as she went upstairs, and round the bend where the barometer hung beneath the stuffed birds. Then he went back to the room, and stood on the hearthrug before the paper fireplace ornament. "Cads!" he said in a scathing undertone, as a fresh burst of laughter came floating in. All through supper he had been composing stinging repartee, a blistering speech of denunciation to be presently delivered. He would rate them as a nobleman should: "Call themselves Englishmen, indeed, and insult a woman!" he would say; take the names and addresses perhaps, threaten to speak to the Lord of the Manor, promise to let them hear from him again, and so out with consternation in his wake. It really ought to be done.

"Teach 'em better," he said fiercely, and tweaked his moustache painfully. What was it? He revived the objectionable remark for his own exasperation, and then went over the heads of his speech again.

He coughed, made three steps towards the door, then stopped and went back to the hearthrug. He wouldn't — after all. Yet was he not a Knight Errant? Should such men go unreproved, unchecked, by wandering baronets *incognito?* Magnanimity? Look at it in that way? Churls beneath one's notice? No; merely a cowardly subterfuge. **He** *would*— after all.

Something within him protested that he was a hot-headed ass even as he went towards the door again. But he only went on the more resolutely. He crossed the hall, by the bar, and entered the room from which the remark had proceeded. He opened the door abruptly and stood scowling on them in the doorway. "You'll only make a mess of it," remarked the internal sceptic. There were five men in the room altogether: a fat person, with a long pipe and a great number of chins, in an armchair by the fireplace, who wished Mr. Hoopdriver a good evening very affably; a young fellow smoking a cutty and displaying crossed legs with gaiters; a little, bearded man with a toothless laugh; a middle-aged, comfortable man with bright eyes, who wore a velveteen jacket; and a fair young man, very genteel in a yellowish-brown ready-made suit and a white tie.

"H'm," said Mr. Hoopdriver, looking very stern and harsh. And then in a forbidding tone, as one who consented to no liberties, "Good evening."

"Very pleasant day we've been 'aving," said the fair young man with the white tie.

"Very," said Mr. Hoopdriver, slowly; and taking a brown armchair, he planted it with great deliberation where he faced the fireplace, and sat down. Let's see — how did that speech begin?

"Very pleasant roads about here," said the fair young man with the white tie.

"Very," said Mr. Hoopdriver, eyeing him darkly. Have to begin somehow. "The roads about here are all right, and the weather about here is all right, but what I've come in here to say is — there's some damned unpleasant people — damned unpleasant people!"

"Oh!" said the young man with the gaiters, apparently making a mental inventory of his pearl buttons as he spoke. "How's that?"

Mr. Hoopdriver put his hands on his knees and stuck out his elbows with extreme angularity. In his heart he was raving at his idiotic folly at thus bearding these lions, — indisputably they *were* lions, — but he had to go through with it now. Heaven send, his breath, which was already getting a trifle spasmodic, did not suddenly give out. He fixed his eye on the face of the fat man with the chins, and spoke in a low, impressive voice. "I came here, sir," said Mr. Hoopdriver, and paused to inflate his cheeks, "with a lady."

"Very nice lady," said the man with the gaiters, putting his head on one side to admire a pearl button that had been hiding behind the curvature of his calf. "Very nice lady indeed."

"I came here," said Mr. Hoopdriver, "with a lady."

"We saw you did, bless you," said the fat man with the chins, in a curious wheezy voice. "I don't see there's anything so very extraordinary in that. One 'ud think we hadn't eyes."

Mr. Hoopdriver coughed. "I came here, sir—"

"We've 'eard that," said the little man with the beard, sharply and went off into an amiable chuckle. "We know it by 'art," said the little man, elaborating the point.

Mr. Hoopdriver temporarily lost his thread. He glared malignantly at the little man with the beard, and tried to recover his discourse. A pause.

"You were saying," said the fair young man with the white tie, speaking very politely, "that you came here with a lady."

"A lady," meditated the gaiter gazer.

The man in velveteen, who was looking from one speaker to another with keen, bright eyes, now laughed as though a point had been scored, and stimulated Mr. Hoopdriver to speak, by fixing him with an expectant regard.

"Some dirty cad," said Mr. Hoopdriver, proceeding with his discourse, and suddenly growing extremely fierce, "made a remark as we went by this door."

"Steady on!" said the old gentleman with many chins. "Steady on! Don't you go a-calling us names, please."

"One minute!" said Mr. Hoopdriver. "It wasn't I began calling names." ("Who did?" said the man with the chins.) "I'm not calling any of you dirty cads. Don't run away with that impression. Only some person in this room made a remark that showed he wasn't fit to wipe boots on, and, with all due deference to such gentlemen as *are* gentlemen"(Mr. Hoopdriver looked round for moral support), "I want to know which it was."

"Meanin'?" said the fair young man in the white tie.

"That I'm going to wipe my boots on 'im straight away," said Mr. Hoopdriver, reverting to anger, if with a slight catch in his throat — than which threat of personal violence nothing had been further from his thoughts on entering the room. He said this because he could think of nothing else to say, and stuck out his elbows truculently to hide the sinking of his heart. It is curious how situations run away with us.

"'Ullo, Charlie!" said the little man, and "My eye!" said the owner of the chins. "You're going to wipe your boots on 'im?" said the fair young man, in a tone of mild surprise.

"I am," said Mr. Hoopdriver, with emphatic resolution, and glared in the young man's face.

"That's fair and reasonable," said the man in the velveteen jacket; "if you can."

The interest of the meeting seemed transferred to the young man in the white tie. "Of course, if you can't find out which it is, I suppose you're prepared to wipe your boots in a liberal way on everybody in the room," said this young man, in the same tone of impersonal question. "This gentleman, the champion lightweight—"

"Own up, Charlie," said the young man with the gaiters, looking up for a moment. "And don't go a-dragging in your betters. It's fair and square. You can't get out of it."

"Was it this—gent?" began Mr. Hoopdriver.

"Of course," said the young man in the white tie, "when it comes to talking of wiping boots—"

"I'm not talking; I'm going to do it," said Mr. Hoopdriver.

He looked round at the meeting. They were no longer antagonists; they were spectators. He would have to go through with it now. But this tone of personal aggression on the maker of the remark had somehow got rid of the oppressive feeling of Hoopdriver *contra mundum*. Apparently, he would have to fight someone. Would he get a black eye?

Would he get very much hurt? Pray goodness it wasn't that sturdy chap in the gaiters! Should he rise and begin? What would she think if he brought a black eye to breakfast to-morrow? "Is this the man?" said Mr. Hoopdriver, with a business-like calm, and arms more angular than ever.

"Eat 'im!" said the little man with the beard; "eat 'im straight orf."

"Steady on!" said the young man in the white tie. "Steady on a minute. If I did happen to say—"

"You did, did you?" said Mr. Hoopdriver.

"Backing out of it, Charlie?" said the young man with the gaiters.

"Not a bit," said Charlie. "Surely we can pass a bit of a joke—"

"I'm going to teach you to keep your jokes to yourself," said Mr. Hoopdriver.

"Bray-vo!" said the shepherd of the flock of chins.

"Charlie *is* a bit too free with his jokes," said the little man with the beard.

"It's downright disgusting," said Hoopdriver, falling back upon his speech. "A lady can't ride a bicycle in a country road, or wear a dress a little out of the ordinary, but every dirty little greaser must needs go shouting insults—"

"*I* didn't know the young lady would hear what I said," said Charlie. "Surely one can speak friendly to one's friends. How was I to know the door was open—"

Hoopdriver began to suspect that his antagonist was, if possible, more seriously alarmed at the prospect of violence than himself, and his spirits rose again. These chaps ought to have a thorough lesson. "Of *course* you knew the door was open," he retorted indignantly. "Of *course* you thought we should hear what you said. Don't go telling lies about it. It's no good your saying things like that. You've had your fun, and you meant to have your fun. And I mean to make an example of you, Sir."

"Ginger beer," said the little man with the beard, in a confidential tone to the velveteen jacket, "is regular up this 'ot weather. Bustin' its bottles it is everywhere."

"What's the good of scrapping about in a public-house?" said Charlie, appealing to the company. "A fair fight without interruptions, now, I *wouldn't* mind, if the gentleman's so disposed."

Evidently the man was horribly afraid. Mr. Hoopdriver grew truculent.

"Where you like," said Mr. Hoopdriver. "Jest wherever you like."

"You insulted the gent," said the man in velveteen.

"Don't be a bloomin' funk, Charlie," said the man in gaiters. "Why, you got a stone of him, if you got an ounce."

"What I say, is this," said the gentleman with the excessive chins, trying to get a hearing by banging his chair arms. "If Charlie goes saying things, he ought to back 'em up. That's what I say. I don't mind his sayin' such things 't all, but he ought to be prepared to back 'em up."

"I'll *back* 'em up all right," said Charlie, with extremely bitter emphasis on 'back.' "If the gentleman likes to come Toosday week—"

"Rot!" chopped in Hoopdriver. "Now."

"'Ear, 'ear," said the owner of the chins.

"Never put off till to-morrow, Charlie, what you can do to-day," said the man in the velveteen coat.

"You got to do it, Charlie," said the man in gaiters. "It's no good."

"It's like this," said Charlie, appealing to everyone except Hoopdriver. "Here's me, got to take in her ladyship's dinner to-morrow night. How should I look with a black eye? And going round with the carriage with a split lip?"

"If you don't want your face sp'iled, Charlie, why don't you keep your mouth shut?" said the person in gaiters.

"Exactly," said Mr. Hoopdriver, driving it home with great fierceness. "Why don't you shut your ugly mouth?"

"It's as much as my situation's worth," protested Charlie.

"You should have thought of that before," said Hoopdriver.

"There's no occasion to be so thunderin' 'ot about it. I only meant the thing joking," said Charlie. "*As* one gentleman to another, I'm very sorry if the gentleman's annoyed —"

Everybody began to speak at once. Mr. Hoopdriver twirled his moustache. He felt that Charlie's recognition of his gentlemanliness was at any rate a redeeming feature. But it became his pose to ride hard and heavy over the routed foe. He shouted some insulting phrase over the tumult.

"You're regular abject," the man in gaiters was saying to Charlie.

More confusion.

"Only don't think I'm afraid, — not of a spindle-legged cuss like him!" shouted Charlie. "Because I ain't."

"Change of front," thought Hoopdriver, a little startled. "Where are we going?"

"Don't sit there and be abusive," said the man

in velveteen. "He's offered to hit you, and if I was him, I'd hit you now."

"All right, then," said Charlie, with a sudden change of front and springing to his feet. "If I must, I must. Now, then!" At that, Hoopdriver, the child of Fate, rose too, with a horrible sense that his internal monitor was right. Things had taken a turn. He had made a mess of it, and now there was nothing for it, so far as he could see, but to hit the man at once. He and Charlie stood six feet apart, with a table between, both very breathless and fierce. A vulgar fight in a public-house, and with what was only too palpably a footman! Good Heavens! And this was the dignified, scornful remonstrance! How the juice had it all happened? Go round the table at him, I suppose. But before the brawl could achieve itself, the man in gaiters intervened. "Not here," he said, stepping between the antagonists. Everyone was standing up.

"Charlie's artful," said the little man with the beard.

"Buller's yard," said the man with the gaiters, taking the control of the entire affair with the easy readiness of an accomplished practitioner. "If the gentleman *don't* mind." Buller's yard, it seemed, was the very place. "We'll do the thing regular and decent, *if* you please." And before he completely realized what was happening, Hoopdriver was being marched out through the back premises of the inn, to the first and only fight with fists that was ever to glorify his life.

Outwardly, so far as the intermittent moonlight showed, Mr. Hoopdriver was quietly but eagerly prepared to fight. But inwardly he was a chaos of conflicting purposes. It was extraordinary how things happened. One remark had trod so closely on the heels of another, that he had had the greatest difficulty in following the development of the business. He distinctly remembered himself walking across from one room to the other, — a dignified, even an aristocratic figure, primed with considered eloquence, intent upon a scathing remonstrance to these wretched yokels, regarding their manners. Then incident had flickered into incident until here he was out in a moonlit lane, — a slight, dark figure in a group of larger, indistinct figures, — marching in a quiet, business-like way towards some unknown horror at Buller's yard. Fists! It was astonishing. It was terrible! In front of him was the pallid figure of Charles, and he saw that the man in gaiters held Charles kindly but firmly by the arm.

"It's blasted rot," Charles was saying, "getting

up a fight just for a thing like that; all very well for 'im. 'E's got 'is 'olidays; 'e 'asn't no blessed dinner to take up to-morrow night like I 'ave.— No need to numb my arm, *is* there?"

They went into Buller's yard through gates. There were sheds in Buller's yard — sheds of mystery that the moonlight could not solve — a smell of cows, and a pump stood out clear and black, throwing a clear black shadow on the whitewashed wall. And here it was his face was to be battered to a pulp. He knew this was the uttermost folly, to stand up here and be pounded, but the way out of it was beyond his imagining. Yet afterwards—? Could he ever face her again? He patted his Norfolk jacket and took his ground with his back to the gate. How did one square? So? Suppose one were to turn and run even now, run straight back to the inn and lock himself into his bedroom? They couldn't make him come out — anyhow. He could prosecute them for assault if they did. How did one set about prosecuting for assault? He saw Charles, with his face ghastly white under the moon, squaring in front of him.

He caught a blow on the arm and gave ground. Charles pressed him. Then he hit with his right and with the violence of despair. It was a hit of his own devising, — an impromptu, — but it chanced to coincide with the regulation hook hit at the head. He perceived with a leap of exultation that the thing his fist had met was the jawbone of Charles. It was the sole gleam of pleasure he experienced during the fight, and it was quite momentary. He had hardly got home upon Charles before he was struck in the chest and whirled backward. He had the greatest difficulty in keeping his feet. He felt that his heart was smashed flat. "Gord darm!" said somebody, dancing toe in hand somewhere behind him. As Mr. Hoopdriver staggered, Charles gave a loud and fear-compelling cry. He seemed to tower over Hoopdriver in the moonlight. Both his fists were whirling. It was annihilation coming — no less. Mr. Hoopdriver ducked perhaps and certainly gave ground to the right, hit, and missed. Charles swept round to the left, missing generously. A blow glanced over Mr. Hoopdriver's left ear, and the flanking movement was completed. Another blow behind the ear. Heaven and earth spun furiously round Mr. Hoopdriver, and then he became aware of a figure in a light suit shooting violently through an open gate into the night. The man in gaiters sprang forward past Mr. Hoopdriver, but too late to intercept the fugitive. There were shouts, laughter, and Mr. Hoopdriver, still solemnly squaring, realized the great and won-

derful truth — Charles had fled. He, Hoopdriver, had fought and, by all the rules of war, had won.

"That was a pretty cut under the jaw you gave him," the toothless little man with the beard was remarking in an unexpectedly friendly manner.

"The fact of it is," said Mr. Hoopdriver, sitting beside the road to Salisbury, and with the sound of distant church bells in his ears, "I had to give the fellow a lesson; simply had to."

"It seems so dreadful that you should have to knock people about," said Jessie.

"These louts get unbearable," said Mr. Hoopdriver. "If now and then we didn't give them a lesson, — well, a lady cyclist in the roads would be an impossibility."

"I suppose every woman shrinks from violence," said Jessie. "I suppose men *are* braver — in a way — than women. It seems to me — I can't imagine — how one could bring oneself to face a roomful of rough characters, pick out the bravest, and give him an exemplary thrashing. I quail at the idea. I thought only Ouida's guardsmen did things like that."

"It was nothing more than my juty — as a gentleman," said Mr. Hoopdriver.

"But to walk straight into the face of danger!"

"It's habit," said Mr. Hoopdriver, quite modestly, flicking off a particle of cigarette ash that had settled on his knee.

THE ABASEMENT OF MR. HOOPDRIVER

XXXIII

On Monday morning the two fugitives found themselves breakfasting at the Golden Pheasant in Blandford. They were in the course of an elaborate doubling movement through Dorsetshire towards Ringwood, where Jessie anticipated an answer from her schoolmistress friend. By this time they had been nearly sixty hours together, and you will understand that Mr. Hoopdriver's feelings had undergone a considerable intensification and development. At first Jessie had been only an impressionist sketch upon his mind, something feminine, active, and dazzling, something emphatically "above" him, cast into his company by a kindly fate. His chief idea, at the outset, as you know, had been to live up to her level, by pretending to be more exceptional, more wealthy, better educated, and, above all, better born than he was. His knowledge of the feminine mind was almost entirely derived from the young ladies he had met in business, and in that class (as in military society and among gentlemen's servants) the good old tradition of a brutal social exclusiveness is still religiously preserved. He had an almost intolerable dread of her thinking him a 'bounder.' Later he began to perceive the distinction of her idiosyncracies. Coupled with a magnificent want of experience was a splendid enthusiasm for abstract views of the most advanced description, and her strength of conviction completely carried Hoopdriver away. She was going to Live her Own Life, with emphasis, and Mr. Hoopdriver was profoundly stirred to similar resolves. So soon as he grasped the tenor of her views, he perceived that he himself had thought as much from his earliest years. "Of course," he remarked, in a flash of sexual pride, "a man is freer than a woman. End in the Colonies, y'know, there isn't half the Conventionality you find in society in this country."

He made one or two essays in the display of unconventionality, and was quite unaware that he impressed her as a narrow-minded person. He suppressed the habits of years and made no proposal to go to church. He discussed church-going in a liberal spirit. "It's jest a habit," he said, "jest a custom. I don't see what good it does you at all, really." And he made a lot of excellent jokes at the chimney-pot hat, jokes he had read in the *Globe* 'turnovers' on that subject. But he showed his gentle breeding by keeping his gloves on all through the Sunday's ride, and ostentatiously throwing away more than half a cigarette when they passed a church whose congregation was gathering for afternoon service. He cautiously avoided literary topics, except by way of compliment, seeing that she was presently to be writing books.

It was on Jessie's initiative that they attended service in the old-fashioned gallery of Blandford church. Jessie's conscience, I may perhaps tell you, was now suffering the severest twinges. She perceived clearly that things were not working out quite along the lines she had designed. She had read her Olive Schreiner and George Egerton, and so forth, with all the want of perfect comprehension of one who is still emotionally a girl. She knew the thing to do was to have a flat and to go to the British Museum and write leading articles for the daily papers until something better came along. If Bechamel (detestable person) had kept his promises, instead of behaving with unspeakable horridness, all would have been well. Now her only hope was that liberal-minded woman, Miss Mergle, who, a year ago, had sent her out, highly educated, into the world. Miss Mergle had told her at parting to live fearlessly and truly, and had further given her a volume of Emerson's Essays and Motley's "Dutch Republic," to help her through the rapids of adolescence.

Jessie's feelings for her stepmother's household at Surbiton amounted to an active detestation. There are no graver or more solemn women in the world than these clever girls whose scholastic advancement has retarded their feminine coquetry. In spite of the advanced tone of 'Thomas Plantagenet's' anti-marital novel, Jessie had speedily seen through that amiable woman's amiable defences. The variety of pose necessitated by the *corps* of 'Men' annoyed her to an altogether unreasonable degree. To return to this life of ridiculous unreality — unconditional capitulation to 'Conventionality' was an exasperating prospect. Yet what else was there to do?

You will understand, therefore, that at times she was moody (and Mr. Hoopdriver respectfully silent and attentive) and at times inclined to eloquent denunciation of the existing order of things. She was a Socialist, Hoopdriver learnt, and he gave a vague intimation that he went further, intending, thereby, no less than the horrors of anarchism. He would have owned up to the destruction of the Winter Palace indeed, had he had the faintest idea where the Winter Palace was, and had his assurance amounted to certainty that the Winter Palace was destroyed.

He agreed with her cordially that the position of women was intolerable, but checked himself on the verge of the proposition that a girl ought not to expect a fellow to hand down boxes for her when he was getting the 'swap' from a customer. It was Jessie's preoccupation with her own perplexities, no doubt, that delayed the unveiling of Mr. Hoopdriver all through Saturday and Sunday. Once or twice, however, there were incidents that put him about terribly — even questions that savoured of suspicion.

On Sunday night, for no conceivable reason, an unwonted wakefulness came upon him. Unaccountably he realised he was a contemptible liar. All through the small hours of Monday he reviewed the tale of his falsehoods, and when he tried to turn his mind from that, the financial problem suddenly rose upon him. He heard two o'clock strike, and three. It is odd how unhappy some of us are at times, when we are at our happiest.

XXXIV

"Good morning, Madam," said Hoopdriver, as Jessie came into the breakfast room of the Golden Pheasant on Monday morning, and he smiled, bowed, rubbed his hands together, and pulled out a chair for her, and rubbed his hands again.

She stopped abruptly, with a puzzled expression on her face. "Where *have* I seen that before?" she said.

"The chair?" said Hoopdriver, flushing.

"No — the attitude."

She came forward and shook hands with him, looking the while curiously into his face. "And — Madam?"

"It's a habit," said Mr. Hoopdriver, guiltily. "A bad habit. Calling ladies Madam. You must put it down to our colonial roughness. Out there — up country — y'know — the ladies — so rare — we call 'em all Madam."

"You *have* some funny habits, brother Chris," said Jessie. "Before you sell your diamond shares and go into society, as you say, and stand for Parliament

—What a fine thing it is to be a man!—you must cure yourself. That habit of bowing as you do, and rubbing your hands, and looking expectant."

"It's a habit."

"I know. But I don't think it a good one. You don't mind my telling you?"

"Not a bit. I'm grateful."

"I'm blessed or afflicted with a trick of observation," said Jessie, looking at the breakfast table. Mr. Hoopdriver put his hand to his moustache and then, thinking this might be another habit, checked his arm and stuck his hand into his pocket. He felt juiced awkward, to use his private formula. Jessie's eye wandered to the armchair, where a piece of binding was loose, and, possibly to carry out her theory of an observant disposition, she turned and asked him for a pin.

Mr. Hoopdriver's hand fluttered instinctively to his lappel, and there, planted by habit, were a couple of stray pins he had impounded.

"What an odd place to put pins!" exclaimed Jessie, taking it.

"It's 'andy," said Mr. Hoopdriver. "I saw a chap in a shop do it once."

"You must have a careful disposition," she said, over her shoulder, kneeling down to the chair.

"In the centre of Africa—up country, that is—

one learns to value pins," said Mr. Hoopdriver, after a perceptible pause. "There weren't over many pins in Africa. They don't lie about on the ground there." His face was now in a fine, red glow. Where would the draper break out next? He thrust his hands into his coat pockets, then took one out again, furtively removed the second pin and dropped it behind him gently. It fell with a loud 'ping' on the fender. Happily she made no remark, being preoccupied with the binding of the chair.

Mr. Hoopdriver, instead of sitting down, went up to the table and stood against it, with his finger-tips upon the cloth. They were keeping breakfast a tremendous time. He took up his rolled serviette, looked closely and scrutinisingly at the ring, then put his hand under the fold of the napkin and examined the texture, and put the thing down again. Then he had a vague impulse to finger his hollow wisdom tooth — happily checked. He suddenly discovered he was standing as if the table was a counter, and sat down forthwith. He drummed with his hand on the table. He felt dreadfully hot and self-conscious.

"Breakfast is late," said Jessie, standing up.

"Isn't it?"

Conversation was slack. Jessie wanted to know the distance to Ringwood. Then silence fell again.

Mr. Hoopdriver, very uncomfortable and studying an easy bearing, looked again at the breakfast things and then idly lifted the corner of the tablecloth on the ends of his fingers, and regarded it. "Fifteen three," he thought, privately.

"Why do you do that?" said Jessie.

"*What?*" said Hoopdriver, dropping the tablecloth convulsively.

"Look at the cloth like that. I saw you do it yesterday, too."

Mr. Hoopdriver's face became quite a bright red. He began pulling his moustache nervously. "I know," he said. "I know. It's a queer habit, I know. But out there, you know, there's native servants, you know, and — it's a queer thing to talk about — but one has to look at things to see, don't y'know, whether they're quite clean or not. It's got to be a habit."

"How odd!" said Jessie.

"Isn't it?" mumbled Hoopdriver.

"If I were a Sherlock Holmes," said Jessie, "I suppose I could have told you were a colonial from little things like that. But anyhow, I guessed it, didn't I?"

"Yes," said Hoopdriver, in a melancholy tone, "you guessed it."

Why not seize the opportunity for a neat confession, and add, "unhappily in this case you guessed wrong." Did she suspect? Then, at the psychological moment, the girl bumped the door open with her tray and brought in the coffee and scrambled eggs.

"I am rather lucky with my intuitions, sometimes," said Jessie.

Remorse that had been accumulating in his mind for two days surged to the top of his mind. What a shabby liar he was!

And, besides, he must sooner or later, inevitably, give himself away.

XXXV

Mr. Hoopdriver helped the eggs and then, instead of beginning, sat with his cheek on his hand, watching Jessie pour out the coffee. His ears were a bright red, and his eyes bright. He took his coffee cup clumsily, cleared his throat, suddenly leant back in his chair, and thrust his hands deep into his pockets. "I'll do it," he said aloud.

"Do what?" said Jessie, looking up in surprise over the coffee pot. She was just beginning her scrambled egg.

"Own up."

"Own what?"

"Miss Milton — I'm a liar."

He put his head on one side and regarded her with a frown of tremendous resolution. Then in measured accents, and moving his head slowly from side to side, he announced, "Ay'm a deraper."

"You're a draper? I thought — "

"You thought wrong. But it's bound to come up. Pins, attitude, habits — It's plain enough.

"I'm a draper's assistant let out for a ten-days

holiday. Jest a draper's assistant. Not much, is it? A counter-jumper."

"A draper's assistant isn't a position to be ashamed of," she said, recovering, and not quite understanding yet what this all meant.

"Yes, it is," he said, "for a man, in this country now. To be just another man's hand, as I am. To have to wear what clothes you are told, and go to church to please customers, and work — There's no other kind of men stand such hours. A drunken bricklayer's a king to it."

"But why are you telling me this now?"

"It's important you should know at once."

"But, Mr. Benson — "

"That isn't all. If you don't mind my speaking about myself a bit, there's a few things I'd like to tell you. I can't go on deceiving you. My name's not Benson. *Why* I told you Benson, I *don't* know. Except that I'm a kind of fool. Well — I wanted somehow to seem more than I was. My name's Hoopdriver."

"Yes?"

"And that about South Africa — and that lion."

"Well?"

"Lies."

"Lies!"

"And the discovery of diamonds on the ostrich

farm. Lies too. And all the reminiscences of the giraffes — lies too. I never rode on no giraffes. I'd be afraid."

He looked at her with a kind of sullen satisfaction. He had eased his conscience, anyhow. She regarded him in infinite perplexity. This was a new side altogether to the man. "But *why*," she began.

"Why did I tell you such things? *I* don't know. Silly sort of chap, I expect. I suppose I wanted to impress you. But somehow, now, I want you to know the truth."

Silence. Breakfast untouched. "I thought I'd tell you," said Mr. Hoopdriver. "I suppose it's snobbishness and all that kind of thing, as much as anything. I lay awake pretty near all last night thinking about myself; thinking what a got-up imitation of a man I was, and all that."

"And you haven't any diamond shares, and you are not going into Parliament, and you're not—"

"All Lies," said Hoopdriver, in a sepulchral voice. "Lies from beginning to end. 'Ow I came to tell 'em I *don't* know."

She stared at him blankly.

"I never set eyes on Africa in my life," said Mr. Hoopdriver, completing the confession. Then he pulled his right hand from his pocket, and with the nonchalance of one to whom the bitterness of death is passed, began to drink his coffee.

"It's a little surprising," began Jessie, vaguely.

"Think it over," said Mr. Hoopdriver. "I'm sorry from the bottom of my heart."

And then breakfast proceeded in silence. Jessie ate very little, and seemed lost in thought. Mr. Hoopdriver was so overcome by contrition and anxiety that he consumed an extraordinarily large breakfast out of pure nervousness, and ate his scrambled eggs for the most part with the spoon that belonged properly to the marmalade. His eyes were gloomily downcast. She glanced at him through her eyelashes. Once or twice she struggled with laughter, once or twice she seemed to be indignant.

"I don't know what to think," she said at last. "I don't know what to make of you — brother Chris. I thought, do you know? that you were perfectly honest. And somehow — "

"Well?"

"I think so still."

"Honest — with all those lies!"

"I wonder."

"I don't," said Mr. Hoopdriver. "I'm fair ashamed of myself. But anyhow — I've stopped deceiving you."

"I *thought*," said the Young Lady in Grey, "that story of the lion — "

"Lord!" said Mr. Hoopdriver. "Don't remind me of *that*."

"I thought, somehow, I *felt*, that the things you said didn't ring quite true." She suddenly broke out in laughter, at the expression of his face. "Of *course* you are honest," she said. "How could I ever doubt it? As if *I* had never pretended! I see it all now."

Abruptly she rose, and extended her hand across the breakfast things. He looked at her doubtfully, and saw the dancing friendliness in her eyes. He scarcely understood at first. He rose, holding the marmalade spoon, and took her proffered hand with abject humility. "Lord!" he broke out, "if you aren't enough — but there!"

"I see it all now." A brilliant inspiration had suddenly obscured her humour. She sat down suddenly, and he sat down too. "You did it," she said, "because you wanted to help me. And you thought I was too Conventional to take help from one I might think my social inferior."

"That was partly it," said Mr. Hoopdriver.

"How you misunderstood me!" she said.

"You don't mind?"

"It was noble of you. But I am sorry," she said, "you should think me likely to be ashamed of you because you follow a decent trade."

"I didn't know at first, you see," said Mr. Hoopdriver.

And he submitted meekly to a restoration of his self-respect. He was as useful a citizen as could be, — it was proposed and carried, — and his lying was of the noblest. And so the breakfast concluded much more happily than his brightest expectation, and they rode out of ruddy little Blandford as though no shadow of any sort had come between them.

XXXVI

As they were sitting by the roadside among the pine trees half-way up a stretch of hill between Wimborne and Ringwood, however, Mr. Hoopdriver reopened the question of his worldly position.

"Ju think," he began abruptly, removing a meditative cigarette from his mouth, "that a draper's shopman *is* a decent citizen?"

"Why not?"

"When he puts people off with what they don't quite want, for instance?"

"Need he do that?"

"Salesmanship," said Hoopdriver. "Wouldn't get a crib if he didn't. — It's no good your arguing. It's not a particularly honest nor a particularly useful trade; it's not very high up; there's no freedom and no leisure — seven to eight-thirty every day in the week; don't leave much edge to live on, does it? — real workmen laugh at us and educated chaps like bank clerks and solicitors' clerks look down on us. You look respectable outside, and inside you are packed in dormitories like convicts, fed on bread and butter and

bullied like slaves. You're just superior enough to feel that you're not superior. Without capital there's no prospects; one draper in a hundred don't even earn enough to marry on; and if he *does* marry, his G. V. can just use him to black boots if he likes, and he daren't put his back up. That's drapery! And you tell me to be contented. Would *you* be contented if you was a shop girl?"

She did not answer. She looked at him with distress in her brown eyes, and he remained gloomily in possession of the field.

Presently he spoke. "I've been thinking," he said, and stopped.

She turned her face, resting her cheek on the palm of her hand. There was a light in her eyes that made the expression of them tender. Mr. Hoopdriver had not looked in her face while he had talked. He had regarded the grass, and pointed his remarks with red-knuckled hands held open and palms upwards. Now they hung limply over his knees.

"Well?" she said.

"I was thinking it this morning," said Mr. Hoopdriver.

"Yes?"

"Of course it's silly."

"Well?"

"It's like this. I'm twenty-three, about. I had my

schooling all right to fifteen, say. Well, that leaves me eight years behind. — Is it too late? I wasn't so backward. I did algebra, and Latin up to auxiliary verbs, and French genders. I got a kind of grounding."

"And now you mean, should you go on working?"

"Yes," said Mr. Hoopdriver. "That's it. You can't do much at drapery without capital, you know. But if I could get really educated. . . . I've thought sometimes . . ."

"Why not?" said the Young Lady in Grey.

Mr. Hoopdriver was surprised to see it in that light. "You think?" he said.

"Of course. You are a Man. You are free—" She warmed. "I wish I were you to have the chance of that struggle."

"Am I Man *enough?*" said Mr. Hoopdriver aloud, but addressing himself. "There's that eight years," he said to her.

"You can make it up. What you call educated men — They're not going on. You can catch them. They are quite satisfied. Playing golf, and thinking of clever things to say to women like my stepmother, and dining out. You're in front of them already in one thing. They think they know everything. You don't. And they know such little things."

"Lord!" said Mr. Hoopdriver. "How you encourage a fellow!"

"If I could only help you," she said, and left an eloquent hiatus. He became pensive again.

"It's pretty evident you don't think much of a draper," he said abruptly.

Another interval. "Hundreds of men," she said, "have come from the very lowest ranks of life. There was Burns, a ploughman; and Hugh Miller, a stonemason; and plenty of others. Dodsley was a footman—"

"But drapers! We're too—sort of shabby genteel to rise. Our coats and cuffs might get crumpled—"

"Wasn't there a Clarke who wrote theology? He was a draper."

"There was one started a sewing cotton, the only one I ever heard tell of."

"Have you ever read 'Hearts Insurgent'?"

"Never," said Mr. Hoopdriver. He did not wait for her context, but suddenly broke out with an account of his literary requirements. "The fact is—I've read precious little. One don't get much of a chance, situated as I am. We have a library at business, and I've gone through that. Most Besant I've read, and a lot of Mrs. Braddon's and Rider Haggard and Marie Corelli—and, well—a Ouida or so. They're good stories, of course, and first-class writers, but they didn't seem to have much to do with me. But there's heaps of books one hears talked about, I *haven't* read."

"Don't you read any other books but novels?"

"Scarcely ever. One gets tired after business, and you can't get the books. I have been to some extension lectures, of course, ' 'Lizabethan Dramatists,' it was, but it seemed a little high-flown, you know. And I went and did wood-carving at the same place. But it didn't seem leading nowhere, and I cut my thumb and chucked it."

He made a depressing spectacle, with his face anxious and his hands limp. "It makes me *sick*," he said, "to think how I've been fooled with. My old schoolmaster ought to have a juiced *hiding*. He's a thief. He pretended to undertake to make a man of me, and he's stole twenty-three years of my life, filled me up with scraps and sweepings. Here I am! I don't *know* anything, and I can't *do* anything, and all the learning time is over."

"Is it?" she said; but he did not seem to hear her.

"My o' people didn't know any better, and went and paid thirty pounds premium — thirty pounds down — to have me made *this*. The G. V. promised to teach me the trade, and he never taught me anything but to be a Hand. It's the way they do with draper's apprentices. If every swindler was locked up — well, you'd have nowhere to buy tape and cotton. It's all very well to bring up Burns and those chaps, but I'm not that make. Yet I'm not such muck that I might not have been better — with teaching. I wonder what the chaps who sneer and laugh at such as me would be if they'd been fooled about as I've been. At twenty-three — it's a long start."

He looked up with a wintry smile, a sadder and wiser Hoopdriver indeed than him of the glorious imaginings. "It's *you* done this," he said. "You're real. And it sets me thinking what I really am, and what I might have been. Suppose it was all different—"

"*Make* it different."

"How?"

"*Work*. Stop playing at life. Face it like a man."

"Ah!" said Hoopdriver, glancing at her out of the corners of his eyes. "And even then—

"No! It's not much good. I'm beginning too late."

And there, in blankly thoughtful silence, that conversation ended.

IN THE NEW FOREST

XXXVII

At Ringwood they lunched, and Jessie met with a disappointment. There was no letter for her at the post office. Opposite the hotel, The Chequered Career, was a machine shop with a conspicuously second-hand Marlborough Club tandem tricycle displayed in the window, together with the announcement that bicycles and tricycles were on hire within. The establishment was impressed on Mr. Hoopdriver's mind by the proprietor's action in coming across the road and narrowly inspecting their machines. His action revived a number of disagreeable impressions, but, happily, came to nothing. While they were still lunching, a tall clergyman, with a heated face, entered the room and sat down at the table next to theirs. He was in a kind of holiday costume; that is to say, he had a more than usually high collar, fastened behind and rather the worse for the weather, and his long-tail coat had been replaced by a black jacket of quite remarkable brevity. He had faded brown shoes on his feet, his trouser legs were grey with dust, and he wore a hat of piebald straw in the place of the customary soft felt. He was evidently socially inclined.

"A most charming day, sir," he said, in a ringing tenor.

"Charming," said Mr. Hoopdriver, over a portion of pie.

"You are, I perceive, cycling through this delightful country," said the clergyman.

"Touring," explained Mr. Hoopdriver.

"I can imagine that, with a properly oiled machine, there can be no easier nor pleasanter way of seeing the country."

"No," said Mr. Hoopdriver; "it isn't half a bad way of getting about."

"For a young and newly married couple, a tandem bicycle must be, I should imagine, a delightful bond."

"Quite so," said Mr. Hoopdriver, reddening a little.

"Do you ride a tandem?"

"No — we're separate," said Mr. Hoopdriver.

"The motion through the air is indisputably of a very exhilarating description." With that decision, the clergyman turned to give his orders to the attendant, in a firm, authoritative voice, for a cup of tea, two gelatine lozenges, bread and butter, salad, and pie to follow. "The gelatine lozenges I must have.

I require them to precipitate the tannin in my tea," he remarked to the room at large, and folding his hands, remained for some time with his chin thereon, staring fixedly at a little picture over Mr. Hoopdriver's head.

"I myself am a cyclist," said the clergyman, descending suddenly upon Mr. Hoopdriver.

"Indeed!" said Mr. Hoopdriver, attacking the moustache. "What machine, may I ask?"

"I have recently become possessed of a tricycle. A bicycle is, I regret to say, considered too — how shall I put it? — *flippant* by my parishioners. So I have a tricycle. I have just been hauling it hither."

"Hauling!" said Jessie, surprised.

"With a shoe lace. And partly carrying it on my back."

The pause was unexpected. Jessie had some trouble with a crumb. Mr. Hoopdriver's face passed through several phases of surprise. Then he saw the explanation. "Had an accident?"

"I can hardly call it an accident. The wheels suddenly refused to go round. I found myself about five miles from here with an absolutely immobile machine."

"'Ow!" said Mr. Hoopdriver, trying to seem intelligent, and Jessie glanced at this insane person.

"It appears," said the clergyman, satisfied with

the effect he had created, "that my man carefully washed out the bearings with paraffin, and let the machine dry without oiling it again. The consequence was that they became heated to a considerable temperature and jammed. Even at the outset the machine ran stiffly as well as noisily, and I, being inclined to ascribe this stiffness to my own lassitude, merely redoubled my exertions."

"'Ot work all round," said Mr. Hoopdriver.

"You could scarcely put it more appropriately. It is my rule of life to do whatever I find to do with all my might. I believe, indeed, that the bearings became red hot. Finally one of the wheels jammed together. A side wheel it was, so that its stoppage necessitated an inversion of the entire apparatus,— an inversion in which I participated."

"Meaning, that you went over?" said Mr. Hoopdriver, suddenly much amused.

"Precisely. And not brooking my defeat, I suffered repeatedly. You may understand, perhaps, a natural impatience. I expostulated — playfully, of course. Happily the road was not overlooked. Finally, the entire apparatus became rigid, and I abandoned the unequal contest. For all practical purposes the tricycle was no better than a heavy chair without castors. It was a case of hauling or carrying."

The clergyman's nutriment appeared in the doorway.

"Five miles," said the clergyman.

He began at once to eat bread and butter vigorously. "Happily," he said, "I am an eupeptic, energetic sort of person — on principle. I would all men were likewise."

"It's the best way," agreed Mr. Hoopdriver, and the conversation gave precedence to bread and butter.

"Gelatine," said the clergyman, presently, stirring his tea thoughtfully, "precipitates the tannin in one's tea and renders it easy of digestion."

"That's a useful sort of thing to know," said Mr. Hoopdriver.

"You are altogether welcome," said the clergyman, biting generously at two pieces of bread and butter folded together.

In the afternoon our two wanderers rode on at an easy pace towards Stoney Cross. Conversation languished, the topic of South Africa being in abeyance. Mr. Hoopdriver was silenced by disagreeable thoughts. He had changed the last sovereign at Ringwood. The fact had come upon him suddenly. Now too late he was reflecting upon his resources. There was twenty pounds or more in the post office savings bank in Putney, but his book was locked up in his box at the Antrobus establishment. Else this infatuated man would certainly have surreptitiously withdrawn the entire sum in order to prolong these journeyings even for a few days. As it was, the shadow of the end fell across his happiness. Strangely enough, in spite of his anxiety and the morning's collapse, he was still in a curious emotional state that was certainly not misery. He was forgetting his imaginings and posings, forgetting himself altogether in his growing appreciation of his companion. The most tangible trouble in his mind was the necessity of breaking the matter to her.

A long stretch up hill tired them long before Stoney Cross was reached, and they dismounted and sat under the shade of a little oak tree. Near the crest the road looped on itself, so that, looking back, it sloped below them up to the right and then came towards them. About them grew a rich heather with stunted oaks on the edge of a deep ditch along the roadside, and this road was sandy; below the steepness of the hill, however, it was grey and barred with shadows, for there the trees clustered thick and tall. Mr. Hoopdriver fumbled clumsily with his cigarettes.

"There's a thing I got to tell you," he said, trying to be perfectly calm.

"Yes?" she said.

"I'd like to jest discuss your plans a bit, y'know."

"I'm very unsettled," said Jessie.

"You are thinking of writing Books?"

"Or doing Journalism, or teaching, or something like that."

"And keeping yourself independent of your stepmother?"

"Yes."

"How long'd it take now, to get anything of that sort to do?"

"I don't know at all. I believe there are a great many women journalists and sanitary inspectors, and black-and-white artists. But I suppose it takes time. Women, you know, edit most papers nowadays, George Egerton says. I ought, I suppose, to communicate with a literary agent."

"Of course," said Hoopdriver, "it's very suitable work. Not being heavy like the drapery."

"There's heavy brain labour, you must remember."

"That wouldn't hurt *you*," said Mr. Hoopdriver, turning a compliment.

"It's like this," he said, ending a pause. "It's a juiced nuisance alluding to these matters, but — we got very little more money."

He perceived that Jessie started, though he did not look at her. "I was counting, of course, on your friend's writing and your being able to take some action to-day." 'Take some action' was a phrase he had learnt at his last 'swop.'

"Money," said Jessie. "I didn't think of money."

"Hullo! Here's a tandem bicycle," said Mr. Hoopdriver, abruptly, and pointing with his cigarette.

She looked, and saw two little figures emerging from among the trees at the foot of the slope. The riders were bowed sternly over their work and made a gallant but unsuccessful attempt to take the rise. The machine was evidently too highly geared for hill climbing, and presently the rearmost rider rose on his saddle and hopped off, leaving his companion to any fate he found proper. The foremost rider was a man unused to such machines and apparently undecided how to dismount. He wabbled a few yards up the hill with a long tail of machine wabbling behind him. Finally, he made an attempt to jump off as one does off a single bicycle, hit his boot against the backbone, and collapsed heavily, falling on his shoulder.

She stood up. "Dear me!" she said. "I hope he isn't hurt."

The second rider went to the assistance of the fallen man.

Hoopdriver stood up, too.

The lank, shaky machine was lifted up and wheeled out of the way, and then the fallen rider, being assisted, got up slowly and stood rubbing his arm.

No serious injury seemed to be done to the man, and the couple presently turned their attention to the machine by the roadside. They were not in cycling clothes Hoopdriver observed. One wore the grotesque raiment for which the Cockney discovery of the game of golf seems indirectly blamable. Even at this distance the flopping flatness of his cap, the bright brown leather at the top of his calves, and the chequering of his stockings were perceptible. The other, the rear rider, was a slender little man in grey.

"Amatoors," said Mr. Hoopdriver.

Jessie stood staring, and a veil of thought dropped over her eyes. She no longer regarded the two men who were now tinkering at the machine down below there.

"How much have you?" she said.

He thrust his right hand into his pocket and produced six coins, counted them with his left index finger, and held them out to her. "Thirteen four half," said Mr. Hoopdriver. "Every penny."

"I have half a sovereign," she said.

"Our bill wherever we stop—" The hiatus was more eloquent than many words.

"I never thought of money coming in to stop us like this," said Jessie.

"It's a juiced nuisance."

"Money," said Jessie. "Is it possible — Surely! Conventionality! May only people of means — Live their own Lives? I never thought . . ."

Pause.

"Here's some more cyclists coming," said Mr. Hoopdriver.

The two men were both busy with their bicycle still, but now from among the trees emerged the massive bulk of a 'Marlborough Club' tandem, ridden by a slender woman in grey and a burly man in a Norfolk jacket. Following close upon this came a lank black figure in a piebald straw hat, riding a tricycle of antiquated pattern with two large wheels in front. The man in grey remained bowed over the bicycle, with his stomach resting on the saddle, but his companion stood up and addressed some remark to the tricycle riders. Then it seemed as if he pointed up hill to where Mr. Hoopdriver and his companion stood side by side. A still odder thing followed; the lady in grey took out her handkerchief, appeared to wave it for a moment, and then at a hasty motion from her companion the white signal vanished.

"Surely," said Jessie, peering under her hand. "It's never — "

The tandem tricycle began to ascend the hill, quartering elaborately from side to side to ease the ascent.

It was evident, from his heaving shoulders and depressed head, that the burly gentleman was exerting himself. The clerical person on the tricycle assumed the shape of a note of interrogation. Then on the heels of this procession came a dogcart driven by a man in a billycock hat and containing a lady in dark green.

"Looks like some sort of excursion," said Hoopdriver.

Jessie did not answer. She was still peering under her hand. "Surely," she said.

The clergyman's efforts were becoming convulsive. With a curious jerking motion, the tricycle he rode twisted round upon itself, and he partly dismounted and partly fell off. He turned his machine up hill again immediately and began to wheel it. Then the burly gentleman dismounted, and with a courtly attentiveness assisted the lady in grey to alight. There was some little difference of opinion as to assistance, she so clearly wished to help push. Finally she gave in, and the burly gentleman began impelling the machine up hill by his own unaided strength. His face made a dot of brilliant colour among the greys and greens at the foot of the hill. The tandem bicycle was now, it seems, repaired, and this joined the tail of the procession, its riders walking behind the dogcart, from which the lady in green and the driver had now descended.

"Mr. Hoopdriver," said Jessie. "Those people — I'm almost sure — "

"Lord!" said Mr. Hoopdriver, reading the rest in her face, and he turned to pick up his machine at once. Then he dropped it and assisted her to mount.

At the sight of Jessie mounting against the sky line the people coming up the hill suddenly became excited and ended Jessie's doubts at once. Two handkerchiefs waved, and some one shouted. The riders of the tandem bicycle began to run it up hill, past the other vehicles. But our young people did not wait for further developments of the pursuit. In another moment they were out of sight, riding hard down a steady incline towards Stoney Cross.

Before they had dropped among the trees out of sight of the hill brow, Jessie looked back and saw the tandem rising over the crest, with its rear rider just tumbling into the saddle. "They're coming," she said, and bent her head over her handles in true professional style.

They whirled down into the valley, over a white bridge, and saw ahead of them a number of shaggy little ponies frisking in the roadway. Involuntarily they slackened. "Shoo!" said Mr. Hoopdriver, and the ponies kicked up their heels derisively. At that Mr. Hoopdriver lost his temper and charged at them, narrowly missed one, and sent them jumping the ditch into the bracken under the trees, leaving the way clear for Jessie.

Then the road rose quietly but persistently; the treadles grew heavy, and Mr. Hoopdriver's breath sounded like a saw. The tandem appeared, making frightful exertions, at the foot, while the chase was still climbing. Then, thank Heaven! a crest and a stretch of up and down road, whose only disadvantage was its pitiless exposure to the afternoon sun. The tandem apparently dismounted at the hill, and did not appear against the hot blue sky until they were already near some trees and a good mile away.

"We're gaining," said Mr. Hoopdriver, with a little Niagara of perspiration dropping from brow to cheek. "That hill—"

But that was their only gleam of success. They were both nearly spent. Hoopdriver, indeed, was quite spent, and only a feeling of shame prolonged the liquidation of his bankrupt physique. From that point the tandem gained upon them steadily. At the Rufus Stone, it was scarcely a hundred yards behind. Then one desperate spurt, and they found themselves upon a steady downhill stretch among thick pine woods. Downhill nothing can beat a highly geared tandem bicycle. Automatically Mr. Hoopdriver put up his feet, and Jessie slackened her pace. In another moment they heard the swish of the fat pneumatics behind them, and the tandem passed Hoopdriver and drew alongside Jessie. Hoopdriver felt a mad impulse to collide with this abominable machine as it passed him. His only consolation was to notice that its riders, riding violently, were quite as dishevelled as himself and smothered in sandy white dust.

Abruptly Jessie stopped and dismounted, and the tandem riders shot panting past them downhill. "Brake!" said Dangle, who was riding behind, and stood up on the pedals. For a moment the velocity of the thing increased, and then they saw the dust fly from the brake, as it came down on the front tire. Dangle's right leg floundered in the air as he came off in the road. The tandem wobbled. "Hold it!" cried Phipps over his shoulder, going on downhill. "I can't get off if you don't hold it." He put on the brake until the machine stopped almost dead, and then feeling unstable began to pedal again. Dangle shouted after him. "Put out your foot, man," said Dangle.

In this way the tandem riders were carried a good hundred yards or more beyond their quarry. Then Phipps realized his possibilities, slacked up with the brake, and let the thing go over sideways, dropping on to his right foot. With his left leg still over the saddle, and still holding the handles, he looked over his shoulder and began addressing uncomplimentary re-

marks to Dangle. "You only think of yourself," said Phipps, with a florid face.

"They have forgotten us," said Jessie, turning her machine.

"There was a road at the top of the hill — to Lyndhurst," said Hoopdriver, following her example.

"It's no good. There's the money. We must give it up. But let us go back to that hotel at Rufus Stone. I don't see why we should be led captive."

So to the consternation of the tandem riders, Jessie and her companion mounted and rode quietly back up the hill again. As they dismounted at the hotel entrance, the tandem overtook them, and immediately afterwards the dogcart came into view in pursuit. Dangle jumped off.

"Miss Milton, I believe," said Dangle, panting and raising a damp cap from his wet and matted hair.

"I *say*," said Phipps, receding involuntarily. "Don't go doing it again, Dangle. *Help* a chap."

"One minute," said Dangle, and ran after his colleague.

Jessie leant her machine against the wall, and went into the hotel entrance. Hoopdriver remained in the hotel entrance, limp but defiant.

AT THE RUFUS STONE

XXXVIII

He folded his arms as Dangle and Phipps returned towards him. Phipps was abashed by his inability to cope with the tandem, which he was now wheeling, but Dangle was inclined to be quarrelsome. "Miss Milton?" he said briefly.

Mr. Hoopdriver bowed over his folded arms.

"Miss Milton within?" said Dangle.

"*And* not to be disturbed," said Mr. Hoopdriver.

"You are a scoundrel, sir," said Mr. Dangle.

"Et your service," said Mr. Hoopdriver. "She awaits 'er stepmother, sir."

Mr. Dangle hesitated. "She will be here immediately," he said. "Here is her friend, Miss Mergle."

Mr. Hoopdriver unfolded his arms slowly, and, with an air of immense calm, thrust his hands into his breeches pockets. Then with one of those fatal hesitations of his, it occurred to him that this attitude was merely vulgarly defiant; he withdrew both, returned one and pulled at the insufficient moustache with the other. Miss Mergle caught him in confusion. "Is this the man?" she said to Dangle, and forthwith, "How *dare* you, sir? How dare you face me? That poor girl!"

"You will permit me to observe," began Mr. Hoopdriver, with a splendid drawl, seeing himself, for the first time in all this business, as a romantic villain.

"Ugh," said Miss Mergle, unexpectedly striking him about the midriff with her extended palms, and sending him staggering backward into the hall of the hotel.

"Let me pass!" said Miss Mergle, in towering indignation. "How dare you resist my passage?" and so swept by him and into the dining-room, wherein Jessie had sought refuge.

As Mr. Hoopdriver struggled for equilibrium with the umbrella-stand, Dangle and Phipps, roused from their inertia by Miss Mergle's activity, came in upon her heels, Phipps leading. "How dare you prevent that lady passing?" said Phipps.

Mr. Hoopdriver looked obstinate, and, to Dangle's sense, dangerous, but he made no answer. A waiter in full bloom appeared at the end of the passage, guardant. "It is men of your stamp, sir," said Phipps, "who discredit manhood."

Mr. Hoopdriver thrust his hands into his pockets.

"Who the juice are you?" shouted Mr. Hoopdriver, fiercely.

"Who are *you*, sir?" retorted Phipps. "Who are *you?* That's the question. What are *you*, and what are you doing, wandering at large with a young lady under age?"

"Don't speak to him," said Dangle.

"I'm not a-going to tell all my secrets to any one who comes at me," said Hoopdriver. "Not Likely." And added fiercely, "And that I tell you, sir."

He and Phipps stood, legs apart and both looking exceedingly fierce at one another, and Heaven alone knows what might not have happened, if the long clergyman had not appeared in the doorway, heated but deliberate. "Petticoated anachronism," said the long clergyman in the doorway, apparently still suffering from the antiquated prejudice that demanded a third wheel and a black coat from a clerical rider. He looked at Phipps and Hoopdriver for a moment, then extending his hand towards the latter, he waved it up and down three times, saying, "Tchak, tchak, tchak," very deliberately as he did so. Then with a concluding "Ugh!" and a gesture of repugnance he passed on into the dining-room from which the voice of Miss Mergle was distinctly audible remarking that the weather was extremely hot even for the time of year.

This expression of extreme disapprobation had a very demoralizing effect upon Hoopdriver, a demoralization that was immediately completed by the advent of the massive Widgery.

"Is this the man?" said Widgery very grimly, and producing a special voice for the occasion from somewhere deep in his neck.

"Don't hurt him!" said Mrs. Milton, with clasped hands. "However much wrong he has done her — No violence!"

"'Ow many more of you?" said Hoopdriver, at bay before the umbrella stand.

"Where is she? What has he done with her?" said Mrs. Milton.

"I'm not going to stand here and be insulted by a lot of strangers," said Mr. Hoopdriver. "So you needn't think it."

"Please don't worry, Mr. Hoopdriver," said Jessie, suddenly appearing in the door of the dining-room. "I'm here, mother." Her face was white.

Mrs. Milton said something about her child, and made an emotional charge at Jessie. The embrace vanished into the dining-room. Widgery moved as if to follow, and hesitated. "You'd better make yourself scarce," he said to Mr. Hoopdriver.

"I shan't do anything of the kind," said Mr. Hoopdriver, with a catching of the breath. "I'm here defending that young lady."

"You've done her enough mischief, I should think," said Widgery, suddenly walking towards the dining-room, and closing the door behind him, leaving Dangle and Phipps with Hoopdriver.

"Clear!" said Phipps, threateningly.

"I shall go and sit out in the garden," said Mr. Hoopdriver, with dignity. "There I shall remain."

"Don't make a row with him," said Dangle.

And Mr. Hoopdriver retired, unassaulted, in almost sobbing dignity.

XXXIX

So here is the world with us again, and our sentimental excursion is over. In the front of the Rufus Stone Hotel conceive a remarkable collection of wheeled instruments, watched over by Dangle and Phipps in grave and stately attitudes, and by the driver of a stylish dogcart from Ringwood. In the garden behind, in an attitude of nervous prostration, Mr. Hoopdriver was seated on a rustic seat. Through the open window of a private sitting-room came a murmur of voices, as of men and women in conference. Occasionally something that might have been a girlish sob.

"I fail to see what status Widgery has," says Dangle, "thrusting himself in there."

"He takes too much upon himself," said Phipps.

"I've been noticing little things, yesterday and to-day," said Dangle, and stopped.

"They went to the cathedral together in the afternoon."

"Financially it would be a good thing for her, of course," said Dangle, with a gloomy magnanimity.

He felt drawn to Phipps now by the common trouble, in spite of the man's chequered legs. "Financially it wouldn't be half bad."

"He's so dull and heavy," said Phipps.

Meanwhile, within, the clergyman had, by promptitude and dexterity, taken the chair and was opening the case against the unfortunate Jessie. I regret to have to say that my heroine had been appalled by the visible array of public opinion against her excursion, to the pitch of tears. She was sitting with flushed cheeks and swimming eyes at the end of the table opposite to the clergyman. She held her handkerchief crumpled up in her extended hand. Mrs. Milton sat as near to her as possible, and occasionally made little dabs with her hand at Jessie's hand, to indicate forgiveness. These advances were not reciprocated, which touched Widgery very much. The lady in green, Miss Mergle (B. A.), sat on the opposite side near the clergyman. She was the strong-minded schoolmistress to whom Jessie had written, and who had immediately precipitated the pursuit upon her. She had picked up the clergyman in Ringwood, and had told him everything forthwith, having met him once at a British Association meeting. He had immediately constituted himself administrator of the entire business. Widgery, having been foiled in an attempt to conduct the proceedings, stood with his legs wide apart in front of the fireplace ornament, and looked profound and sympathetic. Jessie's account of her adventures was a chary one and given amidst frequent interruptions. She surprised herself by skilfully omitting any allusion to the Bechamel episode. She completely exonerated Hoopdriver from the charge of being more than an accessory to her escapade. But public feeling was heavy against Hoopdriver. Her narrative was inaccurate and sketchy, but happily the others were too anxious to pass opinions to pin her down to particulars. At last they had all the facts they would permit.

"My dear young lady," said the clergyman, "I can only ascribe this extravagant and regrettable expedition of yours to the wildest misconceptions of your place in the world and of your duties and responsibilities. Even now, it seems to me, your present emotion is due not so much to a real and sincere penitence for your disobedience and folly as to a positive annoyance at our most fortunate interference —"

"Not that," said Mrs. Milton, in a low tone. "Not that."

"But *why* did she go off like this?" said Widgery. "That's what *I* want to know."

Jessie made an attempt to speak, but Mrs. Milton

said "Hush!" and the ringing tenor of the clergyman rode triumphantly over the meeting. "I cannot understand this spirit of unrest that has seized upon the more intelligent portion of the feminine community. You had a pleasant home, a most refined and intelligent lady in the position of your mother, to cherish and protect you — "

"If I *had* a mother," gulped Jessie, succumbing to the obvious snare of self-pity, and sobbing.

"To cherish, protect, and advise you. And you must needs go out of it all alone into a strange world of unknown dangers — "

"I wanted to learn," said Jessie.

"You wanted to learn. May you never have anything to *un*learn."

"*Ah!*" from Mrs. Milton, very sadly.

"It isn't fair for all of you to argue at me at once," submitted Jessie, irrelevantly.

"A world full of unknown dangers," resumed the clergyman. "Your proper place was surely the natural surroundings that are part of you. You have been unduly influenced, it is only too apparent, by a class of literature which, with all due respect to a distinguished authoress that shall be nameless, I must call the New Woman Literature. In that deleterious ingredient of our book boxes — "

"I don't altogether agree with you there," said

Miss Mergle, throwing her head back and regarding him firmly through her spectacles, and Mr. Widgery coughed.

"What *has* all this to do with me?" asked Jessie, availing herself of the interruption.

"The point is," said Mrs. Milton, on her defence, "that in my books—"

"All I want to do," said Jessie, "is to go about freely by myself. Girls do so in America. Why not here?"

"Social conditions are entirely different in America," said Miss Mergle. "Here we respect Class Distinctions."

"It's very unfortunate. What I want to know is, why I cannot go away for a holiday if I want to."

"With a strange young man, socially your inferior," said Widgery, and made her flush by his tone.

"Why not?" she said. "With anybody."

"They don't do that, even in America," said Miss Mergle.

"My dear young lady," said the clergyman, "the most elementary principles of decorum—A day will come when you will better understand how entirely subservient your ideas are to the very fundamentals of our present civilisation, when you will better understand the harrowing anxiety you have given Mrs. Milton by this inexplicable flight of yours. We can only put things down at present, in charity, to your ignorance — "

"You have to consider the general body of opinion, too," said Widgery.

"Precisely," said Miss Mergle. "There is no such thing as conduct in the absolute."

"If once this most unfortunate business gets about," said the clergyman, "it will do you infinite harm."

"But *I've* done nothing wrong. Why should I be responsible for other people's — "

"The world has no charity," said Mrs. Milton.

"For a girl," said Jessie. "No."

"Now do let us stop arguing, my dear young lady, and let us listen to reason. Never mind how or why, this conduct of yours will do you infinite harm, if once it is generally known. And not only that, it will cause infinite pain to those who care for you. But if you will return at once to your home, causing it to be understood that you have been with friends for these last few days — "

"Tell lies," said Jessie.

"Certainly not. Most certainly not. But I understand that is how your absence is understood at present, and there is no reason — "

Jessie's grip tightened on her handkerchief. "I

won't go back," she said, "to have it as I did before. I want a room of my own, what books I need to read, to be free to go out by myself alone, Teaching—"

"Anything," said Mrs. Milton; "anything in reason."

"But will you keep your promise?" said Jessie.

"Surely you won't dictate to your mother!" said Widgery.

"My stepmother! I don't want to dictate. I want definite promises now."

"This is most unreasonable," said the clergyman.

"Very well," said Jessie, swallowing a sob but with unusual resolution. "Then I won't go back. My life is being frittered away—"

"*Let* her have her way," said Widgery.

"A room then. All your Men. I'm not to come down and talk away half my days—"

"My dear child, if only to save you," said Mrs. Milton.

"If you don't keep your promise—"

"Then I take it the matter is practically concluded," said the clergyman. "And that you very properly submit to return to your proper home. And now, if I may offer a suggestion, it is that we take tea. Freed of its tannin, nothing, I think, is more refreshing and stimulating."

"There's a train from Lyndhurst at thirteen minutes to six," said Widgery, unfolding a time table. "That gives us about half an hour or three-quarters here — if a conveyance is obtainable, that is."

"A gelatine lozenge dropped into the tea cup precipitates the tannin in the form of tannate of gelatine," said the clergyman to Miss Mergle, in a confidential bray.

Jessie stood up, and saw through the window a depressed head and shoulders over the top of the back of a garden seat. She moved towards the door. "While you have tea, mother," she said, "I must tell Mr. Hoopdriver of our arrangements."

"Don't you think I — " began the clergyman.

"No," said Jessie, very rudely; "I don't."

"But, Jessie, haven't you already — "

"You are already breaking the capitulation," said Jessie.

"Will you want the whole half hour?" said Widgery, at the bell.

"Every minute," said Jessie, in the doorway. "He's behaved very nobly to me."

"There's tea," said Widgery.

"I've had tea."

"He may not have behaved badly," said the clergyman. "But he's certainly an astonishingly weak person to let a wrong-headed young girl — "

Jessie closed the door into the garden.

Meanwhile Mr. Hoopdriver made a sad figure in the sunlight outside. It was over, this wonderful excursion of his, so far as she was concerned, and with the swift blow that separated them, he realised all that those days had done for him. He tried to grasp the bearings of their position. Of course, they would take her away to those social altitudes of hers. She would become an inaccessible young lady again. Would they let him say good-bye to her?

How extraordinary it had all been! He recalled the moment when he had first seen her riding, with the sunlight behind her, along the riverside road; he recalled that wonderful night at Bognor, remembering it as if everything had been done of his own initiative. "Brave, brave!" she had called him. And afterwards, when she came down to him in the morning, kindly, quiet. But ought he to have persuaded her then to return to her home? He remembered some intention of the sort. Now these people snatched her away from him as though he was scarcely fit to live in the same world with her. No more he was! He felt he had presumed upon her worldly ignorance in travelling with her day after day. She was so dainty, so delightful, so serene. He began to recapitulate her expressions, the light of her eyes, the turn of her face . . .

He wasn't good enough to walk in the same road with her. Nobody was. Suppose they let him say good-bye to her; what could he say? That? But they were sure not to let her talk to him alone; her mother would be there as, what was it? — *Chaperone.* He'd never once had a chance of saying what he felt; indeed, it was only now he was beginning to realise what he felt. Love! he wouldn't presume. It was worship. If only he could have one more chance. He must have one more chance, somewhere, somehow. Then he would pour out his soul to her — eloquently. He felt eloquently, and words would come. He was dust under her feet . . .

His meditation was interrupted by the click of a door handle, and Jessie appeared in the sunlight under the verandah. "Come away from here," she said to Hoopdriver, as he rose to meet her. "I'm going home with them. We have to say good-bye."

Mr. Hoopdriver winced, opened and shut his mouth, and rose without a word.

XL

At first Jessie Milton and Mr. Hoopdriver walked away from the hotel in silence. He heard a catching in her breath and glanced at her and saw her lips pressed tight and a tear on her cheek. Her face was hot and bright. She was looking straight before her. He could think of nothing to say, and thrust his hands in his pockets and looked away from her intentionally. After a while she began to talk. They dealt disjointedly with scenery first, and then with the means of self-education. She took his address at Antrobus's and promised to send him some books. But even with that it was spiritless, aching talk, Hoopdriver felt, for the fighting mood was over. She seemed, to him, preoccupied with the memories of her late battle, and that appearance hurt him.

"It's the end," he whispered to himself. "It's the end."

They went into a hollow and up a gentle wooded slope, and came at last to a high and open space overlooking a wide expanse of country. There, by a common impulse, they stopped. She looked at her watch — a little ostentatiously. They stared at the billows of forest rolling away beneath them, crest beyond crest, of leafy trees, fading at last into blue.

"The end" ran through his mind, to the exclusion of all speakable thoughts.

"And so," she said, presently, breaking the silence, "it comes to good-bye."

For half a minute he did not answer. Then he gathered his resolution. "There is one thing I *must* say."

"Well?" she said, surprised and abruptly forgetting the recent argument.

"I ask no return. But —"

Then he stopped. "I won't say it. It's no good. It would be rot from me — now. I wasn't going to say anything. Good-bye."

She looked at him with a startled expression in her eyes. "No," she said. "But don't forget you are going to work. Remember, brother Chris, you are my friend. You will work. You are not a very strong man, you know, now — you will forgive me — nor do you know all you should. But what will you be in six years' time?"

He stared hard in front of him still, and the lines about his weak mouth seemed to strengthen. He knew she understood what he could not say.

"I'll work," he said, concisely.

They stood side by side for a moment. Then he said, with a motion of his head, "I won't come back to *them*. Do you mind? Going back alone?"

She took ten seconds to think. "No," she said, and held out her hand, biting her nether lip. "*Good-bye*," she whispered.

He turned, with a white face, looked into her eyes, took her hand limply, and then with a sudden impulse, lifted it to his lips. She would have snatched it away, but his grip tightened to her movement. She felt the touch of his lips, and then he had dropped her fingers and turned from her and was striding down the slope. A dozen paces away his foot turned in the lip of a rabbit hole, and he, stumbled forward and almost fell. He recovered his balance and went on, not looking back. He never once looked back. She stared at his receding figure until it was small and far below her, and then, the tears running over her eyelids now, turned slowly, and walked with her hands gripped hard together behind her, towards Stoney Cross again.

"I did not know," she whispered to herself. "I did not understand. Even now — No, I do not understand."

THE ENVOY

XLI

So the story ends, dear Reader. Mr. Hoopdriver, sprawling down there among the bracken, must sprawl without our prying, I think, or listening to what chances to his breathing. And of what came of it all, of the six years and afterwards, this is no place to tell. In truth, there is no telling it, for the years have still to run. But if you see how a mere counter-jumper, a cad on castors, and a fool to boot, may come to feel the little insufficiencies of life, and if he has to any extent won your sympathies, my end is attained. (If it is not attained, may Heaven forgive us both!) Nor will we follow this adventurous young lady of ours back to her home at Surbiton, to her new struggle against Widgery and Mrs. Milton combined. For, as she will presently hear, that devoted man has got his reward. For her, also, your sympathies are invited.

The rest of this great holiday, too — five days there are left of it — is beyond the limits of our design.

You see fitfully a slender figure in a dusty brown suit and heather mixture stockings, and brown shoes not intended to be cycled in, flitting Londonward through Hampshire and Berkshire and Surrey, going economically — for excellent reasons. Day by day he goes on, riding fitfully and for the most part through bye-roads, but getting a few miles to the north-eastward every day. He is a narrow-chested person, with a nose hot and tanned at the bridge with unwonted exposure, and brown, red-knuckled fists. A musing expression sits upon the face of this rider, you observe. Sometimes he whistles noiselessly to himself, sometimes he speaks aloud, "a juiced good try, anyhow!" you hear; and sometimes, and that too often for my liking, he looks irritable and hopeless. "I know," he says, "I know. It's over and done. It isn't *in* me. You ain't man enough, Hoopdriver. Look at yer silly hands! . . . Oh, my God!" and a gust of passion comes upon him and he rides furiously for a space.

Sometimes again his face softens. "Anyhow, if I'm not to see her — she's going to lend me books," he thinks, and gets such comfort as he can. Then again; "Books! What's books?" Once or twice triumphant memories of the earlier incidents nerve his face for a while. "I put the ky-bosh on *his* little game," he remarks. "I *did* that," and one might

even call him happy in these phases. And, by-the-bye, the machine, you notice, has been enamel-painted grey and carries a sonorous gong.

This figure passes through Basingstoke and Bagshot, Staines, Hampton, and Richmond. At last, in Putney High Street, glowing with the warmth of an August sunset and with all the 'prentice boys busy shutting up shop, and the work girls going home, and the shop folks peeping abroad, and the white 'buses full of late clerks and city folk rumbling home to their dinners, we part from him. He is back. To-morrow, the early rising, the dusting, and drudgery, begin again — but with a difference, with wonderful memories and still more wonderful desires and ambitions replacing those discrepant dreams.

He turns out of the High Street at the corner, dismounts with a sigh, and pushes his machine through the gates of the Antrobus stable yard, as the apprentice with the high collar holds them open. There are words of greeting. "South Coast," you hear; and "splendid weather — splendid." He sighs. "Yes — swapped him off for a couple of sovs. It's a juiced good machine."

The gate closes upon him with a slam, and he vanishes from our ken.

THE END

www.ingramcontent.com/pod-product-compliance
Lightning Source LLC
Chambersburg PA
CBHW022103150426
43195CB00008B/252